Cambridge Elements ≡

Elements in Environmental Humanities

edited by
Louise Westling
University of Oregon
Serenella Iovino
University of North Carolina at Chapel Hill
Timo Maran
University of Tartu

ECOSEMIOTIC LANDSCAPE

A Novel Perspective for the Toolbox of Environmental Humanities

Almo Farina
University of Urbino

CAMBRIDGE
UNIVERSITY PRESS

CAMBRIDGE
UNIVERSITY PRESS

University Printing House, Cambridge CB2 8BS, United Kingdom

One Liberty Plaza, 20th Floor, New York, NY 10006, USA

477 Williamstown Road, Port Melbourne, VIC 3207, Australia

314–321, 3rd Floor, Plot 3, Splendor Forum, Jasola District Centre,
New Delhi – 110025, India

79 Anson Road, #06–04/06, Singapore 079906

Cambridge University Press is part of the University of Cambridge.

It furthers the University's mission by disseminating knowledge in the pursuit of
education, learning, and research at the highest international levels of excellence.

www.cambridge.org
Information on this title: www.cambridge.org/9781108819374
DOI: 10.1017/9781108872928

First published 2021

A catalogue record for this publication is available from the British Library.

ISBN 978-1-108-81937-4 Paperback
ISSN 2632-3125 (online)
ISSN 2632-3117 (print)

Cambridge University Press has no responsibility for the persistence or accuracy of
URLs for external or third-party internet websites referred to in this publication
and does not guarantee that any content on such websites is, or will remain,
accurate or appropriate.

Ecosemiotic Landscape

A Novel Perspective for the Toolbox of Environmental Humanities

Elements in Environmental Humanities

DOI: 10.1017/9781108872928
First published online: January 2021

Almo Farina
University of Urbino
Author for correspondence: Almo Farina, almo.farina@uniurb.it

Abstract: The distinction between humans and the natural world is an artifact and more a matter of linguistic communication than a conceptual separation. This Element proposes ecosemiotics as an epistemological tool to understand better the relationship between human and natural processes. Ecosemiotics, with its affinity to the humanities, is presented here as the best disciplinary approach for interpreting complex environmental conditions for a broad audience, across a multitude of temporal and spatial scales. It is proposed as an intellectual bridge between divergent sciences to incorporate different paradigms within a unique framework. The ecosemiotic paradigm helps to explain how organisms interact with their external environments using mechanisms common to all living beings that capture external information and matter for internal usage. This paradigm can be applied in all the circumstances where a living being (human, animal, plant, fungi, etc.) performs processes to stay alive.

Keywords: complexity, uncertainty, information, ecosemiotics, landscape

ISBNs: 9781108819374 (PB), 9781108872928 (OC)
ISSNs: 2632-3125 (online), 2632-3117 (print)

Contents

1 Introduction

The natural world is overstressed and degraded by growing human intrusion into the majority of ecological processes, reducing their effectiveness (Crutzen & Stoermer 2000). Also, as an agent of ecosystem services, "nature" is not fully represented in human social and cultural contexts dominated by economic and political priorities. Human considerations amount to a diffuse underestimation of life's processes in the entire Earth system, and thus cause weakness in human strategies for preserving natural resources and biodiversity, maintaining ecosystem services, and finally assuring a satisfactory level of well-being to all human societies for the long term.

To try to remediate and reduce this cultural gap, I propose a narrative based on the spirit of Descartes's *catena scientiarum* (Foucher de Careil 1859–1860) in which well-explained rules could identify specific scientific elements to form a shared human understanding. This Element therefore aims to develop a coherent set of ecological and semiotic theories and principles focused on landscape as a fundamental dimension in which environmental and human processes can find coherent life strategies. In particular, this effort offers a reasoned guide to theories, principles, and models that have been proposed recently by scholars from disciplines ranging from ecology, to biosemiotics, ecosemiotics, landscape ecology, and conservation biology as an epistemological model to be placed side-by-side with humanities like anthropology, archeology, history, etc. (Figure 1).

The main arguments to be discussed are:

Complexity (Section 2): Complexity is a universal paradigm that results from interactions of a plethora of abiotic and biotic processes far from equilibrium. These are statistically highly improbable and generate a condition of apparent slowdown of the entropic disorder that Schrodinger (1944) called negentropy, rich with surprise and information (Lloyd 2007). Complexity is the humus on which life blooms, evolves, differentiates, and eventually suffers from extinction in some particular traits and organizational forms. Complexity is necessary to assure continuity for every life form and their functional assemblages on the Earth. At the same time, intra- and interspecific interactions feed turnover and evolution in the composition of biological assemblages.

Uncertainty (Section 3): Uncertainty is a characteristic of the universe that every species must face. It means that unexpected events can occur at any time and cause the possible incapacity of a species when it is exposed to previously unknown risks. At the same time, uncertainty can stimulate processes/mechanisms of adaptation.

Information (Section 4): If complexity is a property that emerges from aggregation and organization across spatial, temporal, and functional scales of organisms, its quantification is represented by the amount of information expressed by the system. Thus, information is the currency exchanged between organisms and their aggregations/assemblages.

Some ecological paradigms (Section 5): The role of ecological paradigms is of first magnitude in my discussion and in particular will be presented using r/K strategies of selection by organisms for survival (Pianka 1970), the source-sink model (Pulliam 1988), and ecological niche theory (Hutchinson 1957). These paradigms have an ecosemiotic counterpart and therefore create the necessary background for an ecosemiotic theory.

The Landscape dimension (Section 6): In the present narrative we consider the landscape as the phenomenological context, the common arena or container in which complexity emerges and differentiates. Landscape is a perfect candidate for this role because it is the spatial, temporal, and cultural context in which different agents (humans, animals, plants, bacteria, viruses) find real possibilities to deeply exchange information with abiotic life support and biotic assemblages. Given that no organisms can escape the perceptive/semiotic mechanisms that link the individual to its surroundings, the concept of landscape is implicit in the definition of life (Barbieri 2008). In particular, the decision to use landscape as the phenomenological context for connecting ecological and semiotic principles is encouraged by the universality with which the landscape processes are considered by all organisms.

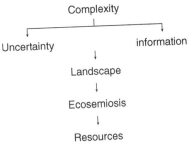

Figure 1 – The main ingredients of landscape ecosemiosis, where Complexity is the main character of systems, include Uncertainty as the constraint that the organism faces, Information as the currency exchanged between the system and organisms for maintaining an active channel of communication, and Landscape as the physical and cognitive spatial dimension. Ecosemiosis is the process of signification, and Resources are material or immaterial entities that nourish life's autopoiesis.

The landscape dimension is based upon the principles of landscape ecology, a relatively young discipline that has gained great popularity since the 1980s (Wu & Hobbs 2007). The multiplicity of visions that have been presented in this discipline pose serious problems of synthesis between different paradigmatic approaches ranging from geographical to semiotic perspectives (Lindstrom et al. 2011).

A general theory of resources (Section 7): After the description of the salient qualities of a landscape, the general theory of resources seeks to explain how resources are necessary for autopoietic processes, i.e. reproduction and self-maintenance. The particularities and role of resources for organisms are obvious, as they represent the necessary fuel for life (Varela & Maturana 1980).

Elements of ecosemiotics (Section 8): "Ecosemiotics studies the role of environmental perception and conceptual categorization in the design, construction, and transformation of environmental structures"(Maran & Kull 2014). Ecosemiotics is the use of a zoosemiotic paradigm that has its fundamentals in biosemiotics, in communication theory, and in animal behavior (Maran et al. 2011, 2016).

We propose that ecosemiosis can function as an intellectual bridge between divergent sciences to incorporate within a unique framework different paradigms born of separate perspectives (Eder & Rembold 1992), and to demonstrate the efficiency and utility of an approach that assures connectedness among signals from different sources.

Ecosemiosis is at the basis of food chains, connecting species to their environments by semethic (semion-sign and ethos-habit) interactions, establishing "personal" reciprocal knowledges among different organisms as they communicate in particular situations (Hoffmeyer 2008, p. 189). Ecosemiosis is responsible for environmental changes produced by these creatures according to their specific sensory abilities.

Human culture is an important agent in these ecosemiotic processes by increasing knowledge between species. However, paradoxically, the diversity that results from communication processes that can accommodate species in close ecological spaces together, may become a risk because of too many communications, or too much noise (Kull 2005).

Fundamentals of ecoacoustics (Section 9): Recently the role of sounds in ecological processes has been emphasized on a theoretical basis in ecoacoustics (Farina 2018a). Sound is a semiotic tool for communication between individuals and species, for navigation (especially in the absence of light), for performance of reproductive behaviors, and for transmission of cultural messages. Soundscapes are the emerging acoustic characteristics of landscapes and impart complexity to environmental systems.

Cultural landscapes (Section 10): Recognizing some landscape configurations as the result of cultural human stewardship associated with historical processes places cultural landscapes in a privileged position. Cognitive, cultural, and spiritual qualities enrich the signs that emerge from landscape. Cultural landscapes maintain a high level of biodiversity resulting from long-term coadaptation of humans with other living beings and demonstrate how the integration of separate concepts as those above is guided by a thinking rooted in the humanities (Smith 2014). A serious attempt to bring natural processes – especially ecological processes – within the purview of the humanities is an activity absolutely necessary to assure the durable and sustainable development of human societies (Eder & Rembold 1992). A new ecosemiotic framework, powered by an integrated epistemology, can forestall a planetary catastrophe created by development based on the doctrine of necessary continuous increase of gross production and from which evident signs of ecosystem degradation and biological impoverishment are growing at an alarming frequency (e.g. Hallmann et al. 2017, Lister & Garcia 2018, Sanchez-Bayo & Wyckhuys 2019). Such ecosystem degradation is also associated with the growing difference of well-being between poor and rich societies and countries.

2 Environmental Complexity: An Ecosemiotic Vision

2.1 Synthesis

Complexity is an emergent property of environmental systems and is associated with their order, diversity, and resilience. Recent human intrusion reduces complexity and thus puts many life forms at risk and compromises human well-being.

Although complexity is an elusive concept, it characterizes the majority of physical, biological, economic, and social systems. It manifests itself at every level of hierarchical scale by which we perceive and describe our known universe. Complexity emerges at the border between different levels of organization and has been compared by Lloyd (1990) to a firebreak that retards the inexorable thermodynamic dissolution of the world.

Complexity is the result of interactions between different scaled systems either in the macrocosm or in the microcosm; energy, matter, and information are its fundamentals. Environmental complexity emerges as a property from intra- and interspecific interactions between individuals, species, and their assemblages, occurring along a broad range of temporal, spatial, and functional scales (Figure 2).

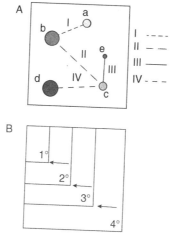

Figure 2 – Schematic representation of complexity: (A) Complexity is created by reserved relationships between different objects (a,b,c,d,e) with a distinct typology of interactions (I,II,III,IV); (B) Complexity emerges at the border between different scaled systems; here are represented four systems inside a hierarchy.

Environmental complexity is the result of the stability, resilience, and diversity of every organized system (Fraccascia et al. 2018, Siegenfeld & Bar-Yam 2019). Complexity is not a self-explicative, visible character; it requires a multidisciplinary approach to be perceived, identified, and finally interpreted (Lewin 1999). Complexity cannot be gauged as an absolute value, but instead by comparing systems with differing levels of organization. An impressive literature around this concept puts the evidence on different systems hierarchically organized. Complexity may be considered a kaleidoscope paradigm because at a micro-level it appears as intricate multifactor relationships, but scaling up, at a macro-level systems seem to respond to a lower number of variables.

The tools for guidance across this scenario are based on the capacity of an observer to intercept and elaborate "the messages" that every life form directly, and the physical contexts indirectly, continuously scatter around. In every system, individual species have a deep exchange of signals with other communicating subjects (Bradbury & Vehrencamp 1998). The quality and quantity of such signals assure their survival or decree their extinction. But a paradox of this paradigm is that the incommunicability between organisms and between systems contributes to complexity and maintains the functionality of ecological systems (Gell-Mann 1995, Gell-Mann & Lloyd 1996).

The human role as environmental keystone species has enormous influence on political, economic, and social decisions that affect the Earth's fate, and thus we need wider and more efficient communication channels with all other organisms (Cristancho & Vining 2004). This process is largely covered by scientific research that tries to fill the information gap between biological/ ecological processes and human cultural agencies (Haines-Young & Potschin 2010). However, achieving this goal requires the incorporation of information from many different fields of scientific research, not as separate contributions but as an integrated and connected "meta-culture" that transcends the boundaries of geography, class, epoch, and social context and can interpret and preserve the Earth's complexity.

The recent human intrusion in natural systems, in geological terms, is a dramatic factor that reduces the complexity of environmental systems, increasing fragility and risk of species extinction.

The complex character of a system also emerges from the combination of knowledge and ignorance, where, in this context knowledge represents the level by which species perceive the processes that are in action outside their physical dimension (body), and ignorance is the amount of external information/processes not sensed and/or not appropriately encoded. Ignorance is a property that creates a sufficient isolation of species by reducing niche space. But ignorance may produce an excess of isolation and then loss of the interconnectedness necessary for the creation of energy chains in the utilization of resources in an interacting community or ecosystem favoring and accelerating entropic processes.

At the same time, ignorance offers advantages because it reduces the number of interactions that could strain the individual biological machine.

The "ecological knowledge and ignorance" are properties common to all living beings, but human intrusion could differently modulate their relative importance and effects.

For instance, human intrusion in food webs may have profound effects on apex predators that, in turn, may have dramatic consequences on the mesopredator's preys (Strong & Frank 2010).

3 Environmental Uncertainty: Contrasting Strategies and Species Adaptation

3.1 Synthesis

Uncertainty is a common experience of the environment for species, caused by the unpredictability of external events or produced by internal processes. For every species, reducing uncertainty is strategic for maintaining the ability to adapt and thus reducing the risk of extinction.

The distribution of energy, materials, and information is neither uniform in space nor constant in time, thus producing a heterogeneous phenomenological space within which species and their assemblages must function. It makes a world full of uncertainty for every biological action. However, every system has a component of uncertainty that alternates with certainty to assure highly predictable processes. For example, a wildfire represents an uncertain process at a relatively small spatial scale, but a fire regime that characterizes and maintains a prairie system in a long-term perspective can be considered a certainty process (Vale 2002). The certainty context is a synonym for the constancy, predictability, and regularity that impart order to a system.

Every organism tries to live in a certain context, avoiding surprises, but often highly improbable events break on the scene and disrupt regularities. Surprise requires an additional expenditure of energy to be neutralized, but facing surprise is also an important exercise for species that activates otherwise latent evolutionary processes. Uncertainty is the measure of the degree to which events are determined by factors out of the range of an individual's knowledge (Templeton & Giraldeau 1995, Dall & Johnstone 2002). The real world is full of improbable patterns and processes. One needs only to think about the unpredictability of weather or the variability of stock prices, where heterogeneity in space and time are two faces of the same coin. But definitively, uncertainty is the context in which environmental complexity develops. The struggle for survival of species is a fundamental Darwinian paradigm (Darwin 1859), but this struggle is primarily motivated by the need for a species to reduce environmental uncertainty. Unpredictability and the resulting surprise create difficulties for species to access resources, thus increasing involuntary intra- and interspecific competition and risk of predation as well.

Living in a variable world means organisms are exposed to a high level of surprises (Figure 3). The appropriate reaction to such surprises requires finding compensatory strategies in the "evolutionary basket," or the birth of new traits able to contend with such surprises in evolutionary time (Merry 1995). There is some evidence that uncertainty can be compensated by an increasing capacity to access resources or by a demographic compensation (r strategy) like in some frogs (MacArthur & Wilson 1967). Such may be possible after the expansion of specific ecological niches (Levins 1968), but this process is expensive in terms of adaptation, and it requires an investment in supplementary biological energy.

Observing the dynamics of the world in a superficial way, every natural thing seems to happen by chance. The same spatial arrangement of wild animals seems not linked to precise rules. But this notion is completely wrong. Organisms around us are continuously seeking to create regular conditions for their lives, reducing uncertainty, gaining knowledge, and preserving it by a genetic and cultural heritage.

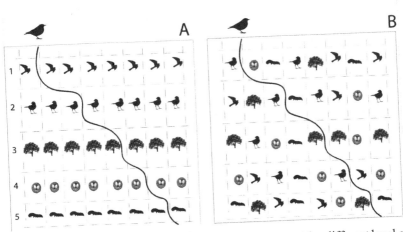

Figure 3 – Hypothetical bird path across two landscapes with a different level of uncertainty: (A) Schematic representation of a landscape at low level of uncertainty, where objects are disposed in a regular way (1: predators; 2: competitors; 3: foraging sites; 4: nesting sites; 5: food) (B) Random distribution of the five typologies of objects met by a species during its habitat navigation across to a landscape of high level of uncertainty.

For example, if we move across an African savanna, it seems that encounters with large herbivores depend on the scouting skills of the local ranger. But in reality, we search for them as we move across an environment, and we discover their presence as we go. The apparent distribution of animals may depend upon our capabilities for following traces and give us the impression of a random world, which has to be sampled or discovered. However, after we have had repeated visits and scouting experiences in the same locations of the African savanna, we become familiar with the surroundings, and our perception of wildness changes. We begin to see that organisms have regular movements and perform repeated behaviors. In other words, the distribution and dynamics of wild animals come to be understood according their individual Umwelt (sensu Von Uexküll 1992).

Every organism tries to create a regular habitat for its life, thus reducing uncertainty and the risk of surprises that cannot be incorporated into its existence. It is not easy to describe how species perceive their environment, but by observing them carefully, we can begin to understand what part of observed reality is perceived by each and what part is invisible/neutral to them. If a bird forages exclusively at the border of a field and never strays far from trees, it means that the open field is perceived as hostile or not suitable for finding food. At the same time, we can follow the tracks of a fox (*Vulpes vulpes*) in the snow, and better understand the olfactory scape of this species and the way it faces uncertainty, the unknown part of a visited territory, internal physiological rhythms, and many other cues as well.

Novelties require a genetic or cultural adaptation in order to be understood, and this demands energy, time, and an investment in morphological adaptation. Often it is believed that a new strategy is needed to face a challenge, but in reality what occurs is not a new strategy but part of an adaptation process that leads to the fixation of new traits.

If people recognize that the world is the result of regular use to track resources, to defend territories, and to reproduce, and that the strategies that people perform to stay alive are the same as those used by all other organisms, we will come close to the solution for living in harmony with all other creatures and avoiding catastrophic epilogues for biodiversity and humanity as well. This reflection should be a point of strength for this Element.

Often organisms structure their life ignoring other species because they are using a different sign system. This "ignorance" can create further novelties and uncertainty. For example, the low resilience of tropical ecosystems is the result of an extreme fine-grained ecological niche resolution (Monacchi & Farina 2019) that produces partitioning of other species living in the same system and thus favors a narrow niche breadth.

Ignorance about other organisms exposes a species to novelties and surprises that in the long term may have a negative impact on individual fitness. Such "ignorance" can be reduced only if perceptive capacities and related mechanisms become common to more species sharing the same environmental experience. This process is a tradeoff between ecological isolation that reduces competition on the one hand, and on the other hand possibilities for operating inside the same eco-semiotic fundamentals (e.g. adopting the same visual, acoustic, or olfactory mechanisms for communication) with benefits in terms of locating resources or cooperating in defense from predators increasing interspecific competition.

4 Information Theory and Meaning

4.1 Synthesis

Information is a polymorphic phenomenon and a polysemantic concept. In a simplified way information may be defined as the difference that makes a difference (Bateson 1970). Information is the currency utilized by every organism in facing the uncertainty produced by environmental dynamics.

4.2 A Short History and Definition

Information is a polymorphic phenomenon and a polysemantic concept used in different fields of knowledge. It is considered to be a basic property of the universe that is organized into a hierarchy of systems (Stonier 1996). Information may also be seen as a convertible coin exchanged between systems at every level of organization, but organisms must use encoding/decoding processes in order to obtain meaning from information (Barbieri 2003).

Information has been defined by Floridi (2010) as a conceptual labyrinth from which escape is not easy. In everyday terms, information can be found in temperature for a lizard, oxygen for a fish, music for a human. As energy is a function of mass or substance, information is a function of the forms of matter. The amount of information is not proportional to mass or energy. For instance, the information in ten copies of the same book is not ten times the information of a single copy. Unlike energy and matter, information does not degrade. For instance, after a book has been read, its information is not depleted and will be the same for a second reader, and so on.

However, the concept of information is not agreed upon by scholars. Its role, ethical use, and abuse are discussed in the philosophy of information (e.g. Adams 2003, Floridi 2010, and Beavers 2016). In a system in which there are two or more possible states, information arises. But it receives different explanations according the level of abstraction utilized (Shannon 1948, 1993), and its importance has been growing during recent decades because of an increase of artificial global connectedness. The concept of information became popular after the advent of telephone networks, computers, and recently, the internet.

Uncertainty may result in damage to species, and the only way to reduce such risk is to continuously gather information from the environment (Dall and Johnstone 2002). This activity, undertaken as quickly as possible, allows identification and assignment of meaning to every object in physical and behavioral contexts. Every species tries to reduce uncertainty by "harvesting" information from such events that are outside the organism's direct control or experience, such as changeable weather conditions and behavior of other organisms (Dall et al. 2005). In this case the information originates in the difference that emerges when two or more patterns based on physical attributes like forms, colors, sounds, or behavioral displays are compared. Like an infinite chain, "information is the difference that makes a difference" (Bateson 1970). Bateson argued that difference is an obscure concept, not a thing or an event, but the distance between two patterns or situations. The Acoustic Complexity Index (Pieretti et al. 2011), one of the most popular, globally accepted metric in ecoacoustics, is based on the measurement of acoustic information as difference between two adjacent values of sound intensity.

4.3 Private and Public Information

Private information is obtained by individual species directly interacting with the environment. Public information, in contrast, is a strategy by which an individual uses information obtained by other individuals and species producing it inadvertently (Valone & Templeton 2002, Danchin et al. 2004). The collection and use of public information saves energy and time, enabling rapid learning about resource depletion, increasing group cohesion. However, it can spread false information as well, as when an entire flock of foraging birds flees when triggered by an overly alarmed individual, without the actual presence of a predator.

Public information reduces the costs/risks of trial-and-error learning, and it feeds the culture that can affect biological evolution. Public information allows organisms to assess the availability and quality of resources, and is used by many species of animals and plants.

Information collected by a conspecific, a member of one's own species, is an important way to locate and assess resources. Such collection and communication of information is an important evolutionary mechanism that helps create complex ecosemiotic systems in which species can select a habitat with fewer resources but close to other members of the species. For example, the house wren (*Troglodytes aedon*), a small bird widely distributed in North America, has a large all-purpose territory but prefers to settle near others of its own kind, instead of choosing isolated territories of equal quality (Muller et al. 1997).

4.4 Abiotic and Biotic Information

Abiotic information is a signal obtained from environmental processes. A dark, cloudy sky is interpreted adaptively by an animal as a proxy for rain.

Biotic information is a sign obtained from an organism. Often animals leave unintentional signals that another individual or species can interpret in order to change its habits. Such information can be accumulated and stored in the environment, where it produces effects for a long time. This exchange of information may have a greater importance than abiotic information. Tracking footprints is a well-known technique in wildlife biology, but very few investigations have been made from an ecosemiotic point of view. Footprint tracking may disclose an important narrative about the way an animal perceives its Umwelt, and about the consequences it may have for other individuals and species after an unintentional release of signals. As an example, Vladimorova and Mozgovoy

(2003) have illustrated a novel approach that transcends the technique of simply following a species. The release of footprints on fresh snow, or on sandy or muddy soils, creates a world of involuntary and unintentional signs that can make the difference for the life of other species. The sign field method proposed by Vladimorova and Mozgovoy enables the rebuilding of the behavioral sequence of an animal, especially on snow and sandy beds where traces are easily stamped. The velocity of walking, the level of interest that a perceived object along the trail produced in the individual being tracked, etc. can be easily annotated and later interpreted by an expert scout. The main characteristics of a sign field have been summarized by Vladimorova and Mozgovoy (2003) as: magnitude, that is, according to the number of different kinds of environmental objects; anisotropy, according to the number of all environmental cues that are perceived by individuals; and intensity, that is, according to the number of elementary movements as responses to environmental cues.

Often the system of such signs remains for a long time in the environment. For instance, large mammals like water buffalo, hippopotamus, crocodiles, and elephants open tracks in forests, savanna, and riparian woodlands that persist for a long time and create ecotonal space and true habitats for many other species. In every environment the modification of the land cover produced by the activity of digging, browsing, etc. generates important signs available for perception and interpretation by other species. These effects are shared from individual to community and by the entire ecosystem. The keystone species concept in ecology is based on this assumption. A keystone species is defined as one whose presence influences the distribution and abundance of other species that have disproportionately large effects on its environment relative to its abundance (Paine 1966, 1969, 1995). And related to this point, emerging knowledge shows that the majority of species modify their own local environment, producing a specific niche for each as an engineer might do (Odling-Smee et al. 2013). Every species tries to acquire optimal knowledge of its habitat and to produce cognitive maps locating resources, avoiding obstacles, and reducing the risk of predation (Healy 1998). Confidence within the environment is necessary for collecting information, because exploration of a new area is costly, not only in terms of energy, but especially also in terms of risk of predation or of risk of starvation caused by lack of information about the distribution of primary resources.

4.5 Meaning and Information

Information can be considered to be a communication process, such as a flux of monetary currency in a bank and where the assumption of a meaning is the destination of such process. Different objects and their spatial arrangement may be "information carriers."

The information generated by a system, but that is not perceived by a recipient, is meaningless information. However, there is a direct relation between meaning and information. Meaning, about which there is an immense literature, is often associated with human elaboration of information, though every animal necessarily links perceived information to a specific meaning (Menant 2003). For instance, an immobile insect is not perceived by a frog as potential prey but probably only an object in the environmental complex. Thus we can speak of a perceived object without any pragmatic semiosis. But when the insect moves, it is perceived as a signal that has the precise meaning of potential prey, so that the frog as predator reacts by trying to swallow. The meaning is the encoding/decoding process applied to information by a receiver (Barbieri 2003, 2019). Other authors couple information to meaning by calling this "meaning information." Reading (2011), for example, defines meaning information as "a pattern of organized matter or energy that is detected by an animate or manufactured receptor and thereby triggers a change in the behavior, functioning, or organizational structure of the detecting entity . . ." Meaning information is generated by matter or energy patterns that have effects on a receiver and produce a change in behavior and physiology. This information depends on the attitude of the recipient. As we shall see later, there is a likeness here with the properties of the interpreted landscape model.

Wiener (1948) distinguished intrinsic information as the level of complexity present inside a living or not living system. Only a few parts of this information are available and detected by a recipient. The transformation of intrinsic information into signals, signs, and messages is the process of creating meaning for a recipient.

Meaningful information belongs to living beings. Although artificial devices can intercept and react with it, these devices do not have the capacity for self-detection and interpretation without specific instructions supplied by human brains.

According to our approach, information is an integral part of ecosemiosis and requires encoding/decoding processes to connect emitter and receiver (Barbieri 2003, p. 15). Patterns of energy and matter detected by a recipient but without the capacity to produce changes in its behavior or physiology are considered merely noise.

4.6 Measuring Information

Given such a plethora of definitions, measuring information seems a difficult task. However, some metrics from information theory can be used; different results can be obtained from particular perspectives. For instance, there is a range of possibilities for measuring the amount of information in five minutes of acoustic chorus created by soniferous species in a tropical forest. We can measure the amount of sound produced within this arbitrary unit of time, or the relative importance of each frequency, or the difference between individual pitches.

Information can thus be measured using the amount and strength of inter-actions between living beings. Its applicability in practice is a formidable solution because of its universality, comparable to numbers in mathematics. Measuring complexity by using information is a common practice because it allows detection of differences in patterns or in processes, and at the same time it can measure the level of improbability or of surprise that occurs in relation-ships between species and along the food chains and abiotic/biotic cycles. Just as electricity is the result of a flux of electrons between two poles characterized by a difference of electric potential, and as electricity may be reversibly used to produce motion, so also information that emerges from the environment and results from the difference among interacting biological organizations can be used by organisms to drive further biological processes.

5 The Role of Ecology in the Ecosemiotic Arena

5.1 Synthesis

The meeting point between ecology and ecosemiotics is deeper and broader than expected. The quantitative approach of ecology in the interpretation of natural phenomena is paired with the semantic approach of ecosemiotics, showing that acting on uncertainty and information can reinterpret r/K adaptation, source/sink dynamics, and ecological niches.

Ecology is a relatively young science that has inherited principles and theories from biology (e.g. Odum 1959, Golley 1993). During its initial development at the beginning of the twentieth century, ecology in Western cultures has been strongly influenced by the cultural separation between natural sciences and the humanities (Brown 1975, 1981), thus fragmenting into several sub-disciplines (e.g. ecosystem ecology (Odum 1983, Real & Brown 1991), landscape ecology (Forman & Godron 1986, Naveh & Lieberman 1996), community ecology (Diamond & Case 1986), individual organisms, and population ecology (Hutchison 1978)). This has restricted the influence of ecology and its impact on human decisions for more than a century, in which economics has dominated the consideration of availability and use of resources. Recent awareness of environmental degradation and the increase of economic and social costs of habitat collapse (Secretariat of the Convention on Biological Diversity 2010) associated with a dramatic reduction of ecosystem services (Costanza et al. 1997) opened the possibility that ecology provide an extraordinary foundation for understanding environmental degradation. For this reason, as Scheiner and Willig (2005, 2011) argue, ecology must be unified according to a more holistic vision of environmental complexity in order to include the contribution offered by environmental humanities.

Operating according to a multiscaled criterion (e.g. from individual to landscape) (sensu Allen & Hoekstra 1992) and adopting an ecosemiotic approach, we find that several ecological principles can intersect to produce an interesting cross-fertilization between ecology and ecosemiotics although the two narratives look separate. Strategies of reproduction (r/K strategies), population dynamics (source-sink model), and ecological niche theory are three examples that have relevant contact in general with complexity and uncertainty paradigms and with ecosemiotics in particular.

5.2 r/K Strategies

In ecology the r/K strategy (MacArthur & Wilson 1967, Pianka 1970) is the adoption of the two modalities, respectively, in an unpredictable environment (r) and in a more predictable environment (K) (Figure 4). Both the mechanisms are based on the principle for guaranteeing reproductive success in species but following completely different paths. The r strategy operates in an ephemeral environment where resources are irregularly distributed, often scarce or available only during short periods. A classical case concerns frog reproduction in temporary ponds where only a few individuals reach the adult stage, from an initial high number of offspring. This strategy serves as response to uncertainty about available resources (e.g. adaptive spawning location, food supply, low risk of predation). With the r strategy a small amount of information (e.g. presence of water) is sufficient for a species to invest in reproduction. But due to great unresolved uncertainty, in spite of the presence of water, other information is collected, and the best strategy is investment in an abnormal release of biomass (i.e. number of eggs). Only by chance will some eggs produce adults in variable habitats. In contrast, species living in stable environments operate a K strategy and have few offspring and a long period of caring for them, resulting in a formidable accumulation of information before and during the reproductive period.

5.3 Source/Sink Model

Assuming that resources are not equally distributed and that habitats may have variable conditions for species, ranging from less to more favorable, the

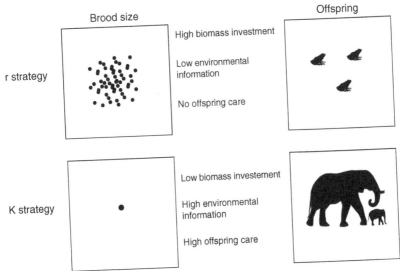

Figure 4 – Ephemeral unpredictable environments require the *r* strategy where a large biomass investment is needed to buffer the high risk of failure. Little ecosemiotic information is sought. Stable environments favor the *K* strategy where, after a low biomass investment, a long period of care guarantees offspring.

source-sink model effectively describes the conditions in which populations living in patches of rich resources (sources) can benefit from favorable reproductive conditions (Figure 5). A surplus of individuals moves continuously from patches rich in resources toward less favorable patches (sink), thus compensating with a continuous replacement for the extinction expected in sink patches (Pulliam 1988). This model finds interesting interrelationships with the perceptive and cognitive criteria used by species in habitat selection. Sink appears to be an ecological trap (Dwernychuk & Boag 1972, Delibes et al. 2001, Battin 2004), and in this case it seems that ecosemiosis is not operating efficiently and that only a population dynamic mechanism can compensate for such an "ecosemiotic mistake" made by a species deceived by habitats that do not provide sufficient resources. It seems difficult to understand why species should prefer less favorable areas, not assessed a priori, in which extinction is their unavoidable fate. One hypothesis might be that apparently for some characteristics, habitats are perceived as suitable for attracting species, but that they are not always reliable indicators of the quantity of available resources. For example, the green carpet of an urban garden attracts birds like the European blackbird (*Turdus merula*) as

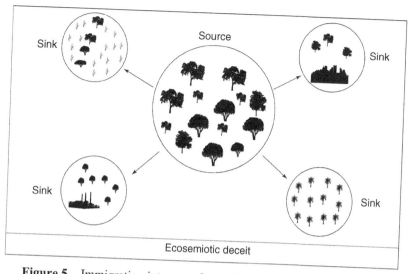

Figure 5 – Immigration into an unfavorable area (sink) is the result of continuous flux of individuals from source areas (native vegetation) favored by a positive demographic balance. Cultivations in periurban and industrialized areas have attractive eco-fields but with a shortage of necessary resources. An ecosemiotic deceit is the origin of this ecological trap.

a preferred site for searching for worms, even in periods of drought when the carpet remains green for some time. During a prolonged drought, however, worms do not emerge at the surface because they have migrated into deep soil. The green carpet in such drought circumstances is simply an ecological trap where ecosemiosis cannot allow access to an unavailable resource of worms.

5.4 Ecological Niche Theory

It is well known that in order to reduce interspecific competition, species try to reduce overlapping demands for common resources. At least two different strategies based on niche theory emerge (Huchinson 1957): one is based on restricted habitat preferences (such species are called "specialists"), and the second is based on species utilization of a broad range of resources (such species are "generalists").

An extraordinary richness of species within a restricted ecological niche is encountered in intertropical regions that benefit from a constancy of environmental fundamentals (e.g. temperature, wind, and rain regime). Intertropical climatic constancy is primarily responsible for the impressive level of biodiversity that is well-documented for plants by Morley (2000), where adaptation to environmental conditions has produced thousands of species that cohabit in restricted habitats.

Although such proliferation of species in intertropical regions has been explained in terms of the constancy of climatic conditions favorable to life, this explanation remains insufficiently supported by a wider geographical comparison of species adaptation in different climatic regimes. The reduction of environmental uncertainty seems one of the most important strategies allowing organisms to adapt and survive. Thus, uncertainty merits a higher ranking among ecological paradigms, a rank too often hidden by more popular paradigms such as "the struggle for survival," a concept that in my opinion is a consequence and not a cause of species actions.

If our reasoning is focused on the level of uncertainty rather than on competition, it emerges that intertropical biomes have a lower level of uncertainty than temperate or boreal biomes because of the well-known astronomical and climatic consequences of the combined inclination and rotation of the planet's axis. Under a regime of low uncertainty, species do not require a great amount of information, and their "Latent Landscape" (see Section 8) is less evolutionarily explored than that of species living in seasonal environments. Definitively a narrow ecosemiotic niche is sufficient to guarantee species survival, but such a species is seen as a specialist with a limited perception of the environment. It will have a high "ignorance" of the environment with a largely unexplored Latent Landscape (Farina 2008). In contrast, a generalist species more tolerant of physical and biological gradients will have a broader niche and greater perceptive and cognitive capacity for collecting information about its surroundings.

Revisiting the r/K strategy, the source-sink model, and ecological niche theory from an ecosemiotic perspective reveals that ecological and ecosemiotic explanations can be collated, contributing to a more exhaustive explanation of observed patterns and processes.

6 Landscape Dimension: Some Relevant Characteristics of Landscape

6.1 Synthesis

Landscapes are physical places composed of mosaics of patches created by the uneven distribution of plants and animals. A landscape is understood as an ecosemiotic system of geographic, ecological, cultural, contemplative, and aesthetic signs and symbols. The landscape is a place in which ecosemiosis can express the more complete linkage between ecological processes and human-related perceptions and interpretations that represents an important model integrating humanities and nature.

Landscape is an emergent level of functional complexity in aquatic and terrestrial environments where matter, energy, information, and semiosis are organized in space (Risser et al. 1984). More generally, landscape may be considered according to a multiplicity of perspectives at the same time: a region, an administrative area, scenery, and a geographical entity where physical units differ in characteristics from one another.

The holistic characteristics expressed by a landscape when it is associated with an ecosemiotic narrative create perfect conditions for shaping a new union between the humans and the natural world. In this way, ecosemiotics can positively influence appropriate environmental policies and promote well-being in human societies (Hoffmeyer 1996, Barrett et al. 2009, Ausonio 2015).

The concept of landscape is recognized by both natural sciences and humanities scholars (Forman & Godron 1986, Farina 1998, Nassauer 1995, Turner et al. 2001, Haber 2004) as one of the best candidates for a rewriting of environmental humanities history in which people and natural processes are finally considered as inseparable ingredients of the Earth's complexity. Such an understanding can launch future development in compliance with environmental sustainability (Lindstrom et al. 2011).

A landscape is composed of physical and cognitive objects delimited by geographical coherences. In particular, a landscape is a mosaic of patches composed of assemblages of plants and animals, with a shape and spatial arrangement resulting from a long succession of disturbance events (Pickett and White 1985). The geographic and contemporarily ecological and cognitive/mental representation of the landscape and the cultural values deposited and stratified there, concur to create a holistic domain in which apparently distant or conflicting concepts like human development and habitat restoration, sustainable use of resources, and human well-being, are integrated and coexist with the growing effects of climate change and the impact of economic policies.

In recent years, the landscape paradigm has been well-developed using ecological theories like hierarchical theory (Allen & Starr 1982), island biogeography theory (MacArthur & Wilson 1967), and metapopulation theory (Hanski 1999), and models like source-sink (Pulliam 1988), ecotones (Holland et al. 1991), and heterogeneity (Kolasa & Pickett 1968).

Every organism interprets common spaces, transforming a landscape into a species-specific living habitat by using processes like perception, elaboration (cognition), communication, and navigation. Our aim is to propose an ecosemiotic approach that describes landscapes in which the geographical space is enriched by the spatial arrangement of cognitively perceived objects. In particular, by focusing on the communication mechanisms within species and between species (intra- and interspecific), we intend to create the conditions for better understanding ecological processes like predator-prey, guild structure, food web complexity, etc.

For instance, investigating an acoustic community, defined as a temporary aggregation of singing animals, enables us to better understand how different species exchange information such as food location and abundance, potential predation, and availability of nesting sites. As another example, the acquisition of information that circulates between shepherd, herding dog, sheep, and vegetation allows a better understanding of the complex interactions at the basis of environmental stability in human-dominated landscapes.

Exploring landscape complexity according to a semiotic perspective means investigating the composition and variety of voluntary or involuntary signals that are exchanged between species, creating a new narrative that can reinforce the bridge between "natural processes" and human life. And, at least in Western cultural traditions, it can restore the lost link between humanities and the environmental sciences. To achieve this goal paradigms, principles, and empirical evidence will be used to shape an epistemological coherence and to discuss the relationships among different perspectives in order to reduce the supposed gap between humans and nature (Vining et al. 2008). This is possible when we realize that humans utilize perceptual tools and operational models also common to other organisms. Investigating the modalities by which organisms communicate with the objects belonging to their habitats is essential for proposing efficient strategies to protect their life and our well-being.

A landscape can be considered according to several conceptualizations simultaneously, as a geographical region, as an ecological entity with the function of a habitat, as a cultural dimension, as a contemplative and an aesthetic location, and finally as an imagined place (Figure 6).

Geography

Ecology

Culture & Aesthetic

Figure 6 – According to different conceptualizations landscape can be considered a container of geographical patterns, ecological processes, cultural heritage, and aesthetic values.

6.2 Landscape as a Geographical Region

The geographical perspective is the result of physical observations of the land, of the distribution of rivers, lakes, glaciers, and so on. This is the most popular identification of landscape. According to this perspective the distribution of developed areas, the organization of cities, and logistical infrastructures are included as well. Landscape is synonymous with territory, region, plain, hills, or mountain range. According to this perspective, a distribution of land forms and related processes like landslides, water falls, erosion, and forest gap sequences depict heterogeneous areas where the evolution of land forms and their biological cover follow a specific storytelling based on different natural disturbance regimes and human interventions.

6.3 Landscape as an Ecological Entity

The landscape conceived as an ecological entity is a vision strongly emphasized by the American school of landscape ecology (Farina 1993), where spatial patterns play a relevant role in ecosystem processes. An ecological landscape is an assemblage of patches of different origin, dynamics, and species composition, where heterogeneity is the dominant character affecting ecological processes, vegetation, and animal patterns (Turner 1987, Kolasa & Pickett 1991). This vision represents the spatially explicit extension of the ecosystem concept (Turner 1989, Forman & Godron 1986, Forman 1995). In association with this perspective, a landscape can be considered also the habitat of species, in which dimension, shape, and distribution of abiotic and biotic components on a spatial matrix concur in shaping the quality of their habitat (Gutzwiller & Anderson 1992, Lidcker 1995, Bissonette 1997).

6.4 Landscape as a Cultural Entity

The landscape can be considered the place in which culture has been developed and dynamically adapted to environmental constraints. Functions and values can be assigned to a landscape according to the local culture, and these are defined as "the customary beliefs, social forms, and material traits of a racial, religious, or social group" but also as "the integrated pattern of human knowledge, belief, and behavior that depends upon the capacity for learning and transmitting knowledge to succeeding generations" (Merriam-Webster dictionary). A landscape in this sense is a unique container of land forms shaped by traditional human activity, reservoir of beliefs and values (Naveh 2003). A landscape is a depositary of stratified ecological events that are fielded by environmental and anthropogenic processes. Such events that pertain to material and unmaterial categories represent a heritage that functions as humus in developing new social and political models, which in turn influence structure and dynamics of ecological processes. The cultural aspect of the landscape will be discussed in Section 10.

6.5 Contemplative and Aesthetic Entity

Coping with the beauty of nature is the intention of land managers, landscape architects, and urbanists. It is difficult to distinguish this perspective from the cultural concept of the landscape, so that it could be considered a subdivision of the former. However, poets, writers, and painters have long considered landscape in terms of scenic views, describing the beauty of nature, its strength, and in some cases its "cruelty" after reports of natural catastrophe, thus focusing on specific signs that seem to have universal value for humans. Landscape aesthetic stimulates many other feelings in people as well, so that the world of imagination finds fertile ground in this dimension, with consequences also on economies (Barrett et al. 2009). In fables the landscape is often described as a location with extraordinary characteristics that provoke surprise, amazement, and fear, or as an enchanted place or a lost paradise.

The landscape dimension is clearly a field of varying human competences according to the perspectives utilized. The multiplicity of possibilities for analysis and assessment created by these perspectives shapes a "multi-dimensional land-scape" that may be represented as a container of distinct "realities" that require trade-off strategies to avoid conflicting uses (Gomez-Sal et al. 2003).

6.6 Landscape Ontogenesis

The mosaic of patches is the result of a stratification of processes that in turn concur to change the land cover. The history of patches (origin and evolution) is known as landscape ontogenesis (Farina and Hong 2004, Farina 2006b, p. 232–234). Empirical evidence reveals that patches originate and/or are affected by at least three different typologies of disturbances that modify their evolution, distribution, and destiny into a land mosaic: processes external to patches (patch novelties), processes between patches (inter-patch competition), and finally processes internal to the individual patches (intra-patch succession) (Figure 7). Such processes have distinct characteristics and modify the land mosaic in various extensions. Energy input and frequency and severity of disturbances are the main factors controlling the entire ontogenetic process. Novelties occur rarely, releasing the maximum energy; inter-patch competition occurs at an intermediate rate of frequency and energy; and intra-patch succes-sion occurs at the highest frequency but demands a lower input of energy.

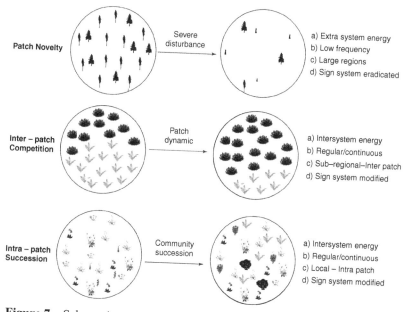

Figure 7 – Schematic representation of landscape ontogenesis that develops according to three stages differentiated in terms of (a) Quantity and source of energy; (b) Frequency of occurrence of the ontogenetic process; (c) Area of competency; (d) Ecosemiotic consequences.

6.6.1 Patch Novelties

Patch novelties are characterized by energy/nutrients coming from external systems like wind, rain storms, or flooding that affect the entire mosaic, reducing the extension of existing patches and/or their internal complexity and creating new patches. Patch novelties modify the mosaic at a large scale like a river catchment. For example, hurricanes can devastate large areas and modify the shape, size, and diversity of the land mosaic for a wide region (Lodge & McDowell 1991).

Patch novelties mobilize a great amount of energy able to severely disrupt the intra- and inter-dynamics of the patches. However, rarely do the novelties have such severe effects that they completely destroy the entire system. One example is the eruption of a volcano, whose lava flow, ashes, and mud may change the land mosaic along the sides and foot of a mountain, but at a large scale natural refuges may survive, ensuring the survival of native species (Dale et al. 2005) and contributing to landscape heterogeneity. Important consequences are evident after a large wildfire like those occurring at growing frequencies in the western and boreal United States (Kitzberger et al. 2017). Burned areas alternate with patches of survivor vegetation at the upwind side of the affected landscape or along land depressions (rivers, streams, canyons) (Dennison et al. 2014).

6.6.2 Inter-patch Competition

Inter-patch competition is the consequence of the ecological constraint/gradient that occurs between patches at different degrees of ecological succession. Inter-patch competition can be considered as ecotonal effects, for instance a neighboring patch of poplar whose fast-growing trees create a situation of shade in an open patch (e.g. meadow), thus changing the composition of vegetation that shifts from sun-tolerant to shade-tolerant.

6.6.3 Intra-patch Succession

Intra-patch succession results from community dynamics. At the scale of an individual patch, patch succession occurs at high frequency in time. The energy and information involved originate in intra-patch processes, and the evolution of intra-patch succession contributes to changes in the physiognomy of individual patches. At the first level of intra-patch succession, the processes that shape the patch are directly conditioned by the internal structure of the patch, by the presence of a diverse collection of seeds, and by its intrinsic heterogeneity.

Patch novelties, inter-patch competition, and intra-patch succession occur repeatedly, and the final result is a mosaic composed of patches originating in these three processes at different impact rates. An ecological succession shapes the patch at any time until other (disturbance) processes coming from neighboring patches or from processes exterior to the system partially or completely disrupt this process.

The resulting mosaic assumes a random configuration largely affected by the amount of energy and information that have circulated. New configurations (composition, shape, spatial arrangement) of patches occur in growing sequence from intra-patch succession to patch novelties. The order/homogeneity of a landscape increases processes from intra-patch succession to patch novelties that operate at a larger spatial scale and at longer temporal recurrences. The memory of the system represents the persistence of a mosaic in time. This is maximum for the patch novelties that influence the entire arrangement of patches deeply and for a long time. Patch novelties, inter-patch competition, and intra-patch succession are rarely fully replaced with new ones at their proper scale, so that they create a mosaic overlapping with the present mosaic, thus increasing randomness especially associated with patch novelties. Landscape is therefore a collection of patches with different histories.

The ecosemiotic consequences of patch novelties, inter-patch competition, and intra-patch succession are of primary importance for animals. These may assist in the partial or total destruction of the sign system developed in their habitats by the establishment of physical markers and familiar perceptual cues, producing an immediate migration/shift of these animals into other patch systems, or in other cases their local extinction.

7 Resources: A General Theory

7.1 Synthesis

Resources are indispensable ingredients for sustaining and complete autopoiesis of species. Their distribution and availability affect presence and abundance of species. Ecosemiotic mechanisms are requested for efficiently tracking resources that are unequally distributed in space and time, and are cryptic in their appearances.

The word "resource" is very popular currently, taking on several different meanings and resulting conceptual changes according to the cultural context in which they appear. The term resource comes from the Latin "resurgere" (re= again) (surgere=spring). This word is applied to physical and biological substances, organisms, and environmental conditions. Different categories can be used to label resources: material such as food, or immaterial such as the aesthetic quality of a landscape. Accordingly their origin can be distinguished as abiotic or biotic. Also their abundance can be seen as limited (like drinkable water) or unlimited (like sunlight or atmospheric nitrogen). Resources can also be ranked according to complexity, such as a simple leaf (according to a caterpillar perspective) or a complex concept like biodiversity (according to a human perspective).

Both material and immaterial resources are indispensable for maintaining life. Matter, energy, information, meaning, and culture can be considered resources across different levels of organization, but without resources life is not possible. Where there are resources, there are organisms. For instance, a colony of penguins can be found where a great amount of fish is available during the critical period of reproduction.

The concept of resources is strictly connected to complexity, uncertainty, and information. The majority of resources are limited and often distributed heterogeneously and this configuration increases uncertainty in organisms. Sunlight that seems an abundant source of energy can be transformed by the shade of tree crowns into a limited resource for plants living in the undergrowth. Similarly, light scarcity is a tremendous barrier for the vertical zonation of aquatic phytoplankton. After a few meters of depth, light is prevented from passing through the water column, so that darkness impedes photosynthesis.

If we search for a common entity able to maintain life, the resource paradigm seems the best candidate, linking ecological processes across temporal and spatial scales. In fact, cells, organisms, populations, communities, ecosystems,

Environmental Humanities

landscapes, biomes, and biosphere – which represent the eight levels of organization that we can distinguish around us (Allen & Oekstra 1992) – have resources as a common requirement to functioning tracked with different modalities according to the level of complexity. Certainly resources are the common denominators of these different levels, where each level exists in the condition to have access to specific resources.

Resources are strictly linked with uncertainty because one is influenced by the other. Scarcity of resources produces an increase of uncertainty, and unpredictability raises difficulties in tracking them. Organisms spend their entire life tracking the necessary resources that substitute components of their bodies, in order to maintain the active flow of internal energy to assist life, to accumulate biomass for the reproductive cycle, and to escape predation.

To track resources, every organism has utilized different strategies in order to unambiguously recognize the necessary resources for its particular needs, thus creating extraordinary semiotic mechanisms that are the basis of such actions as between animal pollinators and plants. In general resources have regular patterns that allow them to be easily located. Some of these patterns are not the result of adaptation, such as the "color" of clean water, but in other cases resources have specific forms and colors for easier identification that results from adaptation processes.

A recent General Theory of Resources (GTR) has interpreted ecological dynamics and created an important link between natural history, societal sciences, and economy (Farina 2012). GTR connects the physical, energetic, and informative components of ecosystems to the semiotic processes of meaning (Nielsen 2007). This theory is based on the 21 axioms of Table 1 above:

1 Resources "spring again" after utilization. This property is particularly relevant because it states a strategic condition for the existence of life. In fact, the energy necessary for completion of regeneration cycles must be continuously provided by an external source like water, light, or nutrients for plants.

2 Due to their uneven distribution in time and space, resources require accurate tracking mechanisms. Central place foraging theory (Stephens & Krebs 1986) demonstrates the adaptability of organisms to cope with the distribution of resources and to organize themselves accordingly. Resource pulses produce immediate concentrations of organisms attracted by the local unexpected abundance of a specific resource (Holt 2008).

3 Often resources adopt cryptic strategies to escape "predators/consumers." There is an impressive literature on this subject. Mimicry and cryptic adaptations seem the two main strategies adopted by some animal and vegetal prey

Table 1 Synthesis of the 21 axioms that create the fundaments of the General Theory

1	Spring again after use
2	Are distributed heterogeneously
3	May have cryptic strategies
4	Semethic relationship exist with the utilizers
5	Regular characters are associated to resource
6	Resources may be necessary, optional, unnecessary
7	Rhythms are consequence of availability after use
8	Need-Function-Semiotic interface is the logic string to track resources
9	The eco-field is the physical ecosemiotic interface between consumer and resource
10	Different eco-fields may overlap without conflicts
11	An eco-field does not guarantee the presence of resource
12	A tradeoff between resource utilization guarantee well-being in the utilizers
13	Resources are direct when a single semiotic process is requested
14	Resources in common create competition between species
15	Resources with a common origin can't be contemporaneously used
16	Umbrella resources open the way in cascade to other resources
17	A neglected resource produces the disappearance of the specific eco-field
18	The expansion of human semiotic niche favors the appearance of new resources
19	Cultural tools are requested to located conceptual resources
20	Habitat is a location where all necessary resources can be intercepted by the utilizers
21	Well-being and ill-being depend by the availability of resources

(resources) to escape predation and consumption (e.g. Ratcliffe & Nydam 2008).

4 The relationship between organisms and resources consists of a type of semethic interaction. The relationship between two organisms, generally is the result of a semethic interaction that establishes a relationship of knowledge between these entities: the first assumes the role of resource for the second (prey/predator, flower/pollinator). This relationship represents a semethis (from semion (sign) + ethos (habit)) interaction: a "personal" reciprocal knowledge (Hoffmeyer 2008). An "affective" relationship is created and maintained between organism and a specific resource after the recognition of the role assumed by the resource. This prerogative transforms a neutral object that can be an organism, some of its parts, or another entity into a resource. For instance, an insect is recognized as prey by a frog only when in motion.

 5 *The appearance of regular characteristics in resources makes finding them easier.* Regular characteristics of the resource facilitate recognition by the "predator/consumer" that uses genetic or cultural mechanisms to track them. Regularity expresses the information at the highest level (Von Barwise & Seligman 1997). Clearly every organism functions better in a "regular" perceived world, while noise and irregularities reduce the possibility of identifying resources and increase environmental uncertainty.

 6 *Distinctive levels of resources: necessary, optional, and unnecessary.* Necessary resources are those whose absence prevents organisms from staying alive or completing their life cycle (e.g. air, water, food, safety).

Optional resources, such as a low diversity of food supply, modify the well-being of an organism. Unnecessary resources are those that do not change the chance of individual survivorship but whose access expands the semiotic niche (e.g. watching a movie for people).

 7 *Resources become available again after previously being depleted for a certain time; we say that they have "invented" rhythms.* Pulses in availability affect individuals and determine the cyclical dynamics of populations and communities (Schwinning & Sala 2004, Holt 2008, Yang et al. 2008). For example, after a period of use and exhaustion, water in a pond in a desert is available to wild and domestic animals only after a period of recharge. The return of availability requires some time that generally becomes characteristic and exclusive of a specific resource and is coped with in the life cycling (rhythms) of the utilizers.

Such is the case for plants browsed by animals like wild or domesticated grazers. Plant regrowth regulates micro- and macro-scale movements of grazing individuals. In traditional agriculture the rotation of fields is performed in order to let the soil recover its fertility after production of a crop; historically it was based on a year-long break from cultivation every several years.

 8 *The String-Need-Function-Semiotic Interface-Resource describes the sequence necessary for tracking resources.* The epistemological framework of this theory foresees a physiologically specific need as an indicator of the level of scarcity of a resource inside the organism. Every need activates a related function (tool) whose role is to find the resource in its physical surroundings using ecosemiotic and cognitive mechanisms. For instance, for a prey organism, escape from predators (a need) requires a searching activity

(function) for a refuge (semiotic interface) in order to acquire safety (resource).

9 A resource is intercepted by a function using a semiotic interface that in most cases has a spatial structure called an eco-field. Functions can be imagined as strings of instructions that activate semiotic mechanisms capable of tracking resources in the surroundings. After they are localized by organism cognitive processes, resources are collected by using specific organs, in the case of a material resource, or by cognitive processes in the case of immaterial ones. For instance, amenity is the immaterial resource searched by people that visit a natural reserve and this resource is absorbed using cognitive processes (knowledge, expectation, scoring, soul enjoying, etc.)

10 Different spatial configuration carriers of meaning (eco-fields) may exist in the same location and thus produce different processes of meaning. Every species has distinct eco-fields for every performed function, which can be associated with others in the same location belonging to other species. A stream of running water could be a place where a fleeing deer could cross and destroy the scent of its tracks, while for a water animal like a beaver that stream could be its home and a place to build a dam and a lodge to protect it from predators.

11 The spatial configuration of a carrier of meaning (eco-field) does not guarantee the presence of a resource but can indicate the context in which a specific resource can be found. Eco-fields are indispensable for tracing resources with a relative saving of energy, but the existence of an eco-field does not guarantee the presence of the associated resource. In such a case the eco-field becomes an ecological trap where organisms do not receive benefits.

12 The availability of resources is not a condition sufficient to guarantee the satisfaction of specific needs, but rather is the trade-off between different resources for determining the final level of well-being. For instance, water holes are obligatory stops in the daily travels of herbivores in arid ecosystems. The necessity of drinking is strongly associated with high risks of predation. It seems that an aggregate presence of different species of herbivores represents a satisfactory trade-off between an increase of interspecific competition, especially when there is a water shortage, and the dilution of the risk of predation in the presence of the aggregation of individuals of different species (Sirot et al. 2016).

13 Resources are called indirect when they are located by the use of more than one process of semiosis. All resources that require at least two processes of semiosis are considered indirect. For example, the majority of therapeutic resources are indirect. These are resources that help people to recover a healthy status after pathologies or periods of severe psychological and physical stress. In order for these therapeutic resources to be located, well-structured semiotic interfaces are necessary. For instance, recreation is an importance resource that can be achieved walking in wilderness. This resource requires a natural and quiet landscape but also a mind free from thoughts.

14 Competition between two species can arise when they have a resource in common that is located by use of the same process of meaning. Territory, reproductive sites, food, etc. create competition between species when the same mechanisms of meaning are used for locating them.

15 When resources have a common origin, their contemporaneous use is not allowed. Many resources originate from a common entity that produces them. For instance tree shade is a resource during the hottest hours of a day for animals living in a tropical savanna (e.g. leopard), but the same trees are also the source of food, leaves, and fruits for other animals (e.g. giraffe). Similarly a tree can produce food for local people, but also wood for cooking fires; the two uses are not possible simultaneously.

16 An umbrella resource is defined by its presence allowing the existence of other derived resources. In ecology, an umbrella species is defined as a species "that needs such large tracts of habitat that saving it will automatically save many other species" (Simberloff 1998). This concept is very popular in biological conservation and can be successfully used to describe the position and role of some (umbrella) resources. Sweet chestnut (*Castanea sativa*) is an important food resource for humans and considered an umbrella resource. To produce and collect this fruit, it is necessary to prune and clear the undergrowth in chestnut orchards. The stewardship of the undergrowth favors palatable grasses for sheep. This grazer encourages voles that represent a resource for owls.

17 When a resource is neglected and no longer identified, it is lost together with its ecosemiotic interface. Especially from a human perspective the disruption of use of a resource (during a cultural shift) often produces its physical or cultural disappearance, followed by the contemporary disappearance of the semiotic interface necessary for its identification.

18 The expansion of the human semiotic niche favors the appearance of new resources, but this process requires new investments to acquire matter, energy, and information. In a difference from other species, humans are able to expand their semiotic niche to capture new resources as suggested by Laland and Brown (2006). The niche construction hypothesis (Odling-Smee et al. 2013) by which every organism modifies its surroundings to improve its living space is particularly useful for describing human expansion across the Earth. Agriculture is the best example of human niche construction, increasing number, variety, and quantity of resources.

19 "Conceptual" resources like biodiversity are difficult to evaluate, and specific cultural tools are needed for their assessment. The generic term "biodiversity" means a collection of organisms and related processes that we value as a resource only after we have evaluated the importance of the redundant processes created by the assemblage of many species in the maintenance of the ecological complexity.

20 A habitat is the ensemble of environmental conditions that allow the presence of resources necessary for a species to stay alive. Habitat is defined by current ecology as a place in which a species lives, characterized by distinct geomorphology, vegetation cover, and distinctive climate (Clement & Shelford 1939). According to resource theory, habitat is considered a spatial container in which a species can find the majority of resources necessary to satisfy its vital functions. The amount of resources determines the quality of a habitat and its source-sink status (Pulliam 1988).

21 Well-being and ill-being are the two opposite conditions that are realized when the resources necessary for maintaining individual autopoiesis are respectively sufficient or insufficient. Access to resources is obligatory for every living being. When all necessary resources are available, organisms enter into the status of well-being. Impediments or unsatisfactory interaction with resources contribute to ill-being. The source-sink paradigm has been used to explain this process using population dynamics according to an ecological perspective.

7.2 Concluding Comments

Resources are required components of the life cycle of every species because they assure energy, matter, and non-physical good and services such as safety and aesthetic resulting in individual well-being. A general theory of resources is useful for better understanding of the central role they play in life itself. Most behavior of organisms is oriented toward tracking resources to feed metabolism and to replace cells in tissues. The growing intrusion of humans in ecosystems associated with consequences like climate change, water and soil acidification, and species extinction, just to list a few, has a strong effect on resources and their dynamics. In a simplified vision, the footprint of resources can be obtained by combining different attributes. Each attribute may be menaced by invasive species, habitat destruction, climate alteration, and phenological alteration. The General Theory of Resources offers an agenda for human development within a context of sustainability.

8 An Ecosemiotic Approach to Landscape Description and Interpretation: From Zoosemiotics to an Eco-field Model

8.1 Synthesis

Behavior and communication (zoosemiosis) are developed by a sequence of signs that compose messages, which are in turn embodied in signals. According to an ecosemiotic perspective, when these processes are contextualized within a geographical space, landscapes become "headquarters" for the majority of information involved in a hierarchy of perceptive and cognitive capacities driven by genetic and cultural factors that are articulated in Latent, Sensed, and Interpreted Landscapes. Signs from a landscape are distinct according to species and by function involved in satisfying a specific need. The eco-field model is invoked as a spatial configuration carrier of meaning necessary for tracking specific resources.

8.2 Elements of Zoosemiotics

The necessity is growing for people to "communicate" with animals in order to prevent the negative effects of their habitat manipulation. According to sacred tradition, Saint Francis of Assisi (1182–1226) had the capacity to communicate directly with animals (Gobry 1959). In one such traditional story, for example, he made a wolf docile.

Today, ethologists have discovered several non-miraculous mechanisms by which it is possible to establish some communication channels between humans and animals. But to understand and interpret animal communication correctly requires a wide variety of scientific disciplines and humanities (e.g. biochemistry, zoology, anatomy, sensory physiology, neurophysiology, comparative psychology, bioacoustics, archaeology, anthropology, linguistics).

According to Thomas Sebeok (1965), the term "zoosemiotics" indicates animal communication not simply as a behavioral process but as the synthesis of an integrated process of information coding and cybernetics. Six aspects can be considered in this process of communication: (1) the source, (2) the destination, (3) a channel, (4) a code, (5) a message, and finally (6) a context. In this process a message is an ordered sequence of signs, and a signal is the physical embodiment of a message.

Perceptual mechanisms are the basis of the sensory capacity of animals. Taste, smell, vision, touch, and hearing are the fundamental senses utilized in animal communication. Visual signals often have a short persistence like flashes. Chemical signals, on the other hand, are the most persistent, and they remain also when the emitter is absent. This has a double benefit: to reduce the risk of being located by predators, and to create a persistent message like a written one, in contrast to an acoustic one that pervades the environment for a few seconds.

There is evident hierarchy in the combined use of signals. For example, a sequence of acoustic, visual, and tactile signals are used by apes and by some birds like parakeets. Ritualization is a further factor in communicative signals that can be defined as behavior redundancy.

In terms of signal efficiency, as already noted, chemical signals are more persistent and have the advantage of depositing a memory across a landscape. Acoustic signals have the advantage of being more independent from physical obstacles and can move quickly and far from sources. Signals used by animals increase in typology and meaning according to the level of evolution. Animals with developed neural systems use signals to transmit complex feelings such as defiance, superiority, friendliness, submission, dejection, etc.

Individual personality is expressed as differences in aggressiveness, shyness, sociability, and activity (Dall et al. 2004). This behavioral complexity is visible in many animals, especially in those living in groups like monkeys and wolves, where social cohesion is part of adaptive strategy.

Semiotic processes are particularly developed in the majority of social animals, where communication is a priority for maintaining the advantage of staying together.

8.3 Encoding Processes

Communication between agents and recipients requires that the signals that emerge from landscapes be transformed into signs by an encoding process that assigns specific meaning (Barbieri 2003). The transition between the information (e.g. perception of an object) and meaning (assignment of a name and the identification of the associated function) is based both on genetic and cultural (neural) codes (Barbieri 2019).

8.4 Landscape Ecosemiotics

Environmental uncertainty is recognized as an important driver of evolutionary processes and contemporarily is the context in which the everyday life of the organism is embedded. The physical arrangement of potential objects that species must identify and classify as neutral, favorable, or unfavorable functions in the landscape as a primary spatial agency. In this narrative, the temporal dimension is also important because a delay in the detection and identification of these objects can make the difference between survival or extinction.

Landscape can be conceived as the semiotic interface between organisms and resources, in which the organism functions as interpreter and represents a reservoir of signs. The landscape can be considered as a depository of cognitive objects whose characteristics are the result of physical perception, mental reworking, and spatial representation, and according to Lindstrom et al. (2014), is analogous to a text. Thus a landscape can be "read" like a text. It is full of signals interpreted according to Saussurean principles as signifier and signified (Saussure 2011), or the objects present in a landscape can be interpreted according to the Peircean triadic semiosis composed of representamen or sign vehicle, object, and interpretant (Buchler 1955).

There is an extensive literature on the human cognitive approach to landscape based on perception theory (Appleton 1996), visual and aesthetic perception (Gibson 1986, Ingold 2000, Bourassa 1991), and psychological perception (Kaplan & Kaplan 1989). Many objects in the landscape can produce visual, thermal, magnetic, tactile, odorous, vibrational, and acoustic information that may be neglected because it is not perceived as a physical constraint/gradient or elaborated using a cognitive mechanism and an encoding procedure that assign specific meanings.

An ideal habitat is one in which every element is well-known by individual species and in which species do not face any uncertainty because they are living inside such "domestic walls." But this model is not easily applicable because the real world is variable and unpredictable. Collecting information from the surrounding environment is strategically necessary for species to maintain chances for survival.

Species adopt varying mechanisms as they try to create well-known Umwelten (sensu von Uexküll 1982, 1992) in which to perform vital functions, reducing at a minimum environmental surprises such as an encounter with a predator, the exhaustion of food stock, confrontation with a new intra- or interspecific competitor, etc.

Landscape as a complex entity is characterized by spatial and temporal heterogeneity, which is perceived and interpreted in a species-specific way by each individual species. Heterogeneity consists of a mosaic of patches or ecotopes, defined as elementary units of a relatively homogeneous landscape, that have distinct internal properties, shape, dimension, and spatial arrangement (Forman 1995) (Figure 8).

It is important to realize that the spatial property of a landscape can be translated from a geographical space to a cognitive space by an encoding/decoding process where individual objects are carriers of different meanings. For instance, a tree may be utilized as a roosting place for a flock of starlings and for this function is selected not only for its dimension and shape but also for its position compared with other plants. The same tree may offer nesting places for tits (*Parus* sp.)

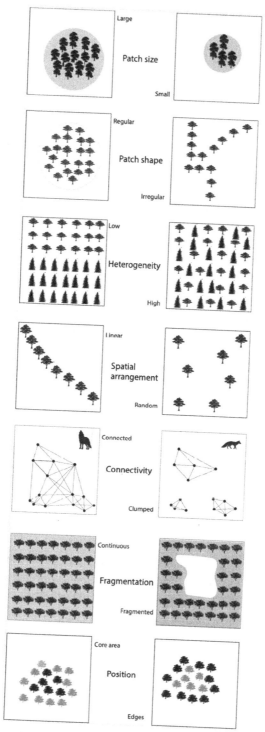

Figure 8 – Emerging patterns (Patch size and shape, Heterogeneity, Spatial arrangement) and processes (Connectivity, Fragmentation, Position) operating in a landscape and interpreted according an ecosemiotic perspective through a coding/decoding process as source of signification.

When food is offered on dishes placed at different distances from a hedgerow, European robins (*Erithacus rubecula*) select the dishes closer to the hedgerow, despite the fact that the dishes have the same shape and the same amount of food supplied. We have called these signs "metric dependent signs" (Farina 2008) that can be distinguished from nonmetric signs such as icons and symbols. As another example, sound that changes in intensity according to the perceived distance from the source is a metric sign. According to the distance, a species can perceive a sign as a strong threat, a reasonable threat, or merely neutral. Acoustic degradation is thus a metric sign process if it is reread according to an ecosemiotic perspective.

Species have the capacity to evaluate the distance from which the acoustic signal is uttered, and thus to decide which behavior to adopt. This capacity is called "ranging." A close acoustic signal may create alarm, but at some distance it may be ignored. We find this in the case of the Carolina wren (*Thyrothorus ludovicianus*) that reacts preferably with undegraded calls (Morton et al. 1986, Morton 1987). With the chaffinch (*Fringilla coelebs*) Naguib et al. (2000) have observed a ranging capacity in individuals exposed to playback experiments simulating singing birds at distances of 0, 20, 40, 80 and 120 meters.

8.5 The Type of Signs that are springing from a Landscape

Landscape is the source for almost all signals available for animals. However, not all the signals are converted into signs, and some signals are apparently too confusing to be interpreted at first sight. In natural sciences, dichotomous keys are commonly used to identify plants, animals, and fungi. Such identification is based on specific characteristics that can be distinguished within a reasonable margin of error. Each organism has characteristics that enable it to be distinguished by others, such as footprints or the iris in the human eye, shape of leaves, structure of flowers, distribution and typology of hairs in plants, teeth and shape of the skull in micromammals, color of feathers, or length of tarsus in birds. Focusing on morphological differences allows us to distinguish the majority of species. However, sibling species require a more sophisticated investigation, such as by DNA analysis. But when we are looking at landscape resolution, it is really difficult to distinguish two different patches of woodland or two meadows. Although it is possible with reasonable certainty to assign a name to every plant, it is practically impossible to assign a name to a landscape by looking only at all individual components at the same time, because a landscape is not simply a collection of land forms, plants, and animals. The spatial abundance and arrangement of patches in a composition create an interacting combination of several possibilities, like the positions of chess pieces. This difficulty is created by the scale of resolution at which the landscape is sensed and interpreted (by people in this case). If the spatial scale is enlarged, details on individual plants vanish, and as with an impressionistic picture, we can appreciate only rough emergent characteristics of the entire visually perceived landscape (e.g. color, shape). In other words, when the resolution according to which objects are observed is modified, details of the previous resolution are lost and new details emerge. For instance, if we observe a meadow from a few meters away, it is possible to detect individual plants. A botanist would be able to assign the scientific names to the species. But at some few meters of greater distance, individual species can no longer be distinguished, and plants appear in the form of patches of different shapes and colors for which the attribution of names is not easy. In a rural landscape it is possible to distinguish an olive grove from a lucerne field, as distinct ecotopes (the smallest ecologically distinct landscape features), but nature creates fuzzier systems that often vanish, one into the other, without evident thresholds of discontinuity.

Signals that emerge from ecotopes may pertain to a higher level of cognitive perception. In humans such signals may be related to feelings such as sadness, happiness, mystery, fear, or wonder. These feelings are probably not so distinguishable in other animals, but we cannot be sure that some of these supposedly human feelings are not also experienced by animals.

A continuous flow of information emerges from a landscape. The source of emission may be of physical origin like the clouds of ash from an erupting volcano, blowing wind, waterfalls, or rain. Each of these elements contributes to differentiate potential signals for a biological receiver. Moreover, the receiver may have a secondary role as the emitter of further information, becoming in turn, as in a chain, a resource (prey) for a highest consumer (predator).

It is not surprising that the perception of a landscape varies according to species and that not all physical elements (patterns: shapes, colors, spatial arrangements; and processes: light, thermal, acoustic waves) of a landscape are perceived and interpreted by organisms in the same ways. Every species has a restricted field of competences that are the result of genetic adaptation formalized into an ecological niche breadth. Definitively Farina et al. (2005) have presented three perceptual landscapes with which species interact with their Umwelten: a Latent Landscape, a Sensed Landscape, and an Interpreted Landscape (Figure 9).

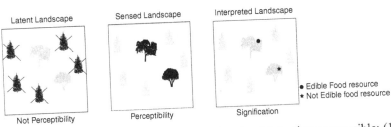

Figure 9 – In landscape ecosemiosis three levels of detection are possible: (1) The Latent Landscape represents the invisible species-specific part of a landscape; (2) the Sensed Landscape is the perceived component; and (3) the Interpreted Landscape is the part that receives a species-specific meaning. In this example, a Latent Landscape is composed of pines, the Sensed Landscape by broadleaf trees, and the Interpreted Landscape is represented by edible and inedible fruits for hypothetical consumers.

8.6 Latent Landscape

The Latent Landscape is composed of "signals" that are not perceived by a species because its sensory abilities are not able to intercept them. All organisms are embedded in a dimension in which some signals are "invisible." For example, thermal patches of soil are sensed by snakes, but these thermal qualities escape human detection. Such a species-specific invisible landscape is called a Latent Landscape. Every new signal that a species can perceive during the course of its evolution is the result of a causal modification of its sensory capacities, guided by instructions filed in the genome. A species-specific Latent Landscape is the source for new adaptations and thus has a fundamental role as an arena in which evolution can take place.

A new capacity can be stabilized through population dynamics according to the level of benefit received. More information can be tracked from the environment and more survival chances offered to an organism by this means. A Latent Landscape is a condition where new sources of information are prevented from being sensed without the emergence of new sensorial capacities resulting from genetic mutations. As an example, humans cannot hear the majority of calls used by bats to locate flying prey, because they are emitted above the range of human hearing capacity that is 22 kHz, or the infrasounds (<20 Hz) emitted by some species of whales. The same is true for the polarization of the light that guides honey bees and several other insects in the exploration of their landscapes and in their homing flights, but that cannot be perceived by humans.

Although the Latent Landscape paradigm was proposed in 2006 (Farina 2006b), similar reasoning was presented by Lloyd (1990) 16 years before, in reporting the example of the bacterium *Escherichia coli* that has an immense capacity to process information under conditions of stress imposed by its surroundings, adapting in a few generations to a new landscape and disclosing and converting part of the Latent Landscape into a Sensed Landscape.

In people the transformation of pieces of a Latent Landscape into a Sensed Landscape is very slow, because the genome is protected by technological, cultural, and ethical shields. This fixity in the genome and its slow evolution are compensated by the expansion of the semiotic niche by which "new technologies process and exchange information in our behalf.... For, after all, a species stumped by an intractable problem does not merely cease to compute. It ceases to exist" (Lloyd 1990). This is the story of biological extinction. When an organism has no genetic possibility for expanding its sensory abilities, for instance when a species has no ability to change its physiological status in response to an increase in temperature, it will become extinct in a short time. In the case of a species living in a cold climate such as the European snow vole (*Chionomys nivalis*), a mountain vole, a rise in temperature will cause extinction if the vole cannot acquire a genetic tolerance to bring a physiological change in its metabolism so that it can adapt to a new thermal regime.

8.7 Sensed Landscape

This landscape results from individual-species perception obtained by the sensory organs (smell, touch, hearing, sight, taste). Sensory abilities vary according to species and are regulated by physiological thresholds. The threshold of perception has conceptual foundations similar to niche theory (Grinnell 1917) and is the result of individual adaptation during evolutionary time by the fixation of functional thresholds. Working above or below a threshold of tolerance causes a species to be exposed to unfavorable conditions that decrease their fitness.

According to this model a landscape is a distribution of environmental gradients perceived by the senses similar to a nuanced coloring in which the distance between upper and lower edges is described as niche breadth (e.g. Pianka 1986). Perceptual capacity is fixed in the genome.

When we investigate aggregations beyond the individual species level (e.g. population, metapopulation, community), other mechanisms can compensate for the constraints imposed by environmental conditions and by the sensitivity of the species. For instance, the source-sink model or the r/K selection are two mechanisms that overpass the rigidity of species-specific physiological/eco-logical requirements, shifting the entire problem to mechanisms of population dynamics.

8.8 Interpreted Landscape

The level of perception in the Interpreted Landscape results from the assignment of a meaning to the objects sensed. Genetic, cognitive, and cultural mechanisms are used by species operating at this level. Evidence suggests that animals can incorporate spatial representations during their life cycle (Real 1993).

In the Interpreted Landscape, the information obtained from the Sensed Landscape is associated with a specific meaning that can be species specific, individual specific, or shared by a wider range of observers.

The culture of an individual can make the difference in terms of the meaning process. This mechanism associated with human cognition is common to other animals like apes and birds (Dukas 1998). For instance, every person can distinguish between a breeze and a strong wind, but only local people have specific names for the perceived wind, such as "foehn," "mistral," or "tradewind," and know the expected duration and consequences for local climate. Snow cover is recognized by everyone, but only indigenous inhabitants of arctic regions are able to distinguish particular types of snow and ice. The linguistic diversity adopted by some aboriginal populations results from detailed discrimination among patterns of very common and persistent phenomena. The cultural distinction of living and nonliving things is finalized according to their use or avoidance. A systematic scientific approach often opens the way to a description of patterns, like the shape and color of caterpillars, which in many cases are not associated with visible functions or meaning.

There is a fundamental distinction between the diversity of languages adopted by aboriginal populations and the categorizations made by science. In aboriginal languages every word used to name a living or nonliving object is originated by its associated cultural function. By contrast, in the majority of scientific characterization and classification, only the physical characteristics (e.g. shape, dimension, color, or region) are used to assign a name to the object.

8.9 The Eco-field Model

The mechanisms of perception are species specific according to the organism, and the survey of surroundings is repeated for every function that a species performs during its life cycle.

In the human dimension, landscape perception depends on the goal pursued, and largely on the spirit with which a person looks around. Subjectivity is very high and depends on individual feeling experienced at a specific moment. The cognitive interpretations of different categories of observers assign different natural, cultural, and economic values to the same landscape. For instance, a marshland is a wild area of high value for eco-tourists, but is perceived by farmers as a hostile environment or badlands, requiring "reclamation" to achieve the standard of rural productivity.

A landscape, in which an ecosemiotic perspective based on an organismic-centered view assigns the role of ecosemiotic agency, is a common home where every species in turn recognizes only parts as eligible characteristics. In fact, the landscape is a container of separate species-specific perceived and interpreted "worlds" or Umwelten, where ecosemiotic mechanisms create permanent communication channels between each species and the environment. This communication channel has been refined by the theory of eco-fields (Farina 2000). The term eco-field, a contraction of "ecological field," is defined as a spatial configuration of "objects" perceived in a coherent way according to functions triggered by needs and carriers of meaning. Species return/assign a meaning to a specific spatial arrangement associated with resources. Conceptually close to the idea of the Umwelt (von Uexküll 1982, 1992), an eco-field is more than a subjective species-specific surrounding because it is a spatial configuration of objects to which ecosemiotic processes guided by internal needs attribute meaning for a specific resource (Figure 10).

Every resource is associated with a specific eco-field, which emerges as a coherent perceptual unit only when a need has activated a function. We can say that a landscape is perceived according to separate ecosemiotic processes guided by internal needs. A hungry bird will explore a landscape according to a searching image, a cognitive template, necessary for intercepting food. Or a lion will decide to attack a herd of gazelles only when gazelles are spaced at distances from each other that create a pattern coincident with a cognitive template that emerges after the need for food has

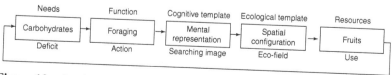

Figure 10 – A schematic representation of ecosemiotic passages that start with needs (e.g. carbohydrates) to obtain a specific resource (fruits).

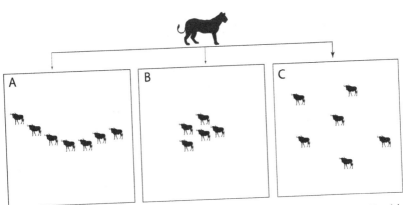

Figure 11 – Different spatial arrangement of a herd of wildebeest: (A) Herd in movement (linear), (B) Herd in defensive behavior (clumped), (C) Herd grazing (sparse). Between these three spatial configurations, only configuration C, when wildebeest are foraging and consequently are more vulnerable, triggers the attack of hunting lions.

activated the lion hunting function (Figure 11). For every internal need there is a cognitive template that is used to scan around in search of a corresponding configuration of objects that are associated semiotically with a specific resource.

The eco-field is a conceptualization that in traditional ecology is largely equivalent to the ecological niche paradigm. Obtaining ecological isolation would seem the best way to reduce competition. However, this is only partially true. In fact some environmental characteristics are perceived in the same way for more than one species, creating a common overlapped perception. This mechanism is not a contraction of the niche concept but represents a further possibility offered by evolutionary forces for allocating knowledge common to more species in the same "place". Finally, in more evolved animals, individuals belonging to the same species may have different capacities for perceiving their surroundings.

In summary the eco-field assumes that:

(1) A species perceives differently scaled characteristics of the environment according to the functional trait activated by a specific physiological requirement (need).

(2) Landscape attributes are sensed and recognized only according to the function that is active at that time.

(3) Environmental suitability is the result of the number of eco-fields present in a location.

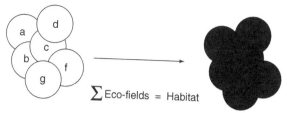

$\sum$ Eco-fields = Habitat

Figure 12 – The entire collection of eco-fields recognized by a species coincides with its habitat.

(4) Priorities in energy intake and integration with other survival mechanisms produce a continuous shift from one species-specific eco-field to another as an organism inspects in this way the resource availability offered by the habitat.

(5) Local extinction, adaptation, and geographical displacement (for mobile organisms) are determined by the emerging suitability or scarcity of the different eco-fields.

(6) The assignment of a specific meaning to a spatial configuration of objects is guided by a multiplicity of mechanisms, of which the first is a physiological need caused by the scarcity of some substance, which triggers a function.

(7) The activation of a function modifies the meaning of the perceived surroundings and an associated searching image is used to scan the objects there.

(8) From an ecosemiotic perspective, a habitat is the portion of a landscape where a species finds the eco-fields for the necessary resources (Figure 12, 13).

8.10 Private and Public Landscape

It is evident that every organism has a peculiar perception of the landscape that enables it to perceive an exclusive, "private" landscape. When shared with other species, this perception belongs to a public landscape (Farina 2006a) that represents the common perception and assignment of meaning between two or more individuals and species. This common landscape plays an important role in population and community aggregation and regulation, offering stability and coherence, and creating a "common culture." For instance, a public landscape may be at the origin of the acoustic communities (Farina and James 2016) in which members of a temporary aggregation based on acoustic communication receive information from the other interspecific partners in the community. Species may receive benefits for sharing part of the habitat information with other species in terms of common anti-predatory behavior and resource tracking. In human societies this phenomenon is at the basis of local community

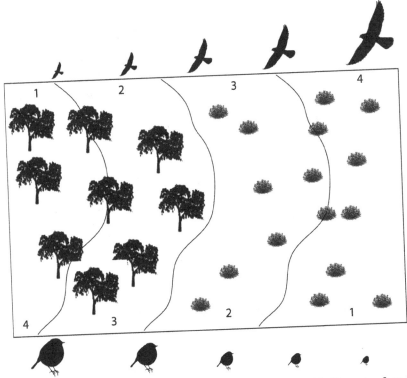

Figure 13 – Example of a fuzzy perception of safety eco-fields (from 4 safe to 1 unsafe position) of European robins (*Erithacus rubecula*) and of hunting eco-fields for sparrow hawks (*Accipter nisus*) from 4 (successful) to 1 (unsuccessful hunting area).

differentiation, well-represented by the birth of customs, traditions, and dialects.

The sum of public and private landscape may be considered as the total Sensed Landscape that can be represented as a perceptual interface between organisms and their resources. The total perceived landscape has characteristics that change according to the species present in an area.

Considering that every species modifies the habitat in which it lives and interferes with several cycles, we can expect an increase in environmental complexity and uncertainty, because every species is responsible for a local disturbance process that can be represented by grazing regimes for herbivorous animals, digging regimes for fossorial animals, etc. This biological disturbance rearranges many components of a landscape and may be responsible for the availability of resources for other species. In fact, a substantial difference between the ecosystem approach and the landscape ecosemiotic approach for investigating environmental complexity is due to the share by species of a common, public landscape. In the landscape ecosemiotic approach, with the introduction of the public versus the private landscape, cognitive objects are highlighted that are shared by different species and can produce changes in interspecific relationships.

9 Fundamentals of Ecoacoustics: A New Quantitative Contribution to the Ecosemiotic Narrative

9.1 Synthesis

Sound is a relevant component of animal communication, and an honest signal is an extraordinary ecosemiotic tool that guarantees primary functions for species like mating, territorial control, social interactions, and navigation. The interpretation of sounds created in landscapes by physical processes (geophonies), animals (biophonies), and human technology (technophonies) helps species to select acoustic habitats. Sounds increase the efficiency of intra- and interspecific communication and in particular reinforce the flux of information and meaning between species and the environment.

Landscape is rich with signals from living and nonliving sources where visual cues (shape, colors, behavioral display) are considered dominant interacting components for assuring intra- and interspecific communication between species. Nevertheless, sounds from physical processes and living organisms represent an ecosemiotic context of primary importance for a great number of animals and plants in terrestrial and aquatic landscapes, confirming their relevance for environmental complexity (Busnel 1968). Acoustic emissions that are optimized during communication processes, like other environmental characteristics, greatly influence life traits of all organisms. Sounds play a fundamental role not only in communication but also in habitat selection and in navigation as well.

Sound is information that flows from emitters to receivers, creating a complex and dynamic semiotic network (McGregor et al. 1997) and assumes a relevant role in several biological processes like navigation (Griffin & Hopkins 1974) and orientation (Radford et al. 2014, Parmentier et al. 2015). Theme, variation, motif, repetition, and intensity of signals contribute to the acoustic information.

Using acoustic cues, organisms track material (e.g. food) and immaterial (e.g. territorial delimitation) resources. The majority of bird songs are associated with territory defense, courtship, and mating (Catchpole & Slater 2008). For example, willow tits (*Poecile montanus*) produce special calls when discovering food, thus attracting conspecific and heterospecific individuals to the food site (Suzuki 2012).

Sound is a type of structured energy that is emitted by elastic bodies, which propagates in the air at 331 m/s at 0°C, and five times faster (1484 m/s) in water but not in a constant way, because sound transmission strongly depends on the physical characteristics of the medium (temperature, salinity, shape of surfaces, pressure, etc.) and by position and distance of emitters compared with the position of receivers. These physical and biological factors play an important role in terms of quality and efficiency of the acoustic signals transmitted. Air and water are two particularly efficient media for transmitting acoustic signals, but soil and solid materials can also transmit acoustic waves in the form of vibrations.

Animal sounds produced by different organs (e.g. vocal chords in mammals, syrinx in birds, vocal sacs in frogs, timbale in cicadas, etc.) are called biophonies, and the species that emit sound are called soniferous. Sounds produced by mechanical devices are called technophonies. Sounds of abiotic origins like those produced by volcanoes, flowing water, marine waves and currents, wind flow, earthquakes, marine ice melting, and thunderstorms are called geophonies. The combination of sounds of different origins create a sonic context or soundscape (Pijanowski et al. 2011a, 2011b).

Soniferous species invest considerable energy during their acoustic performances, as for example during pairing selection in the reproductive period. This is in direct relationship with the status of their health. In fact, biophonies are honest signals because they are reliable indicators of the health levels of organisms (Buchanan et al. 1999, 2002). During evolution species have differentiated their acoustic emissions to reduce frequency overlap and possible confusion between acoustic signals. Thus some species such as dolphins, whales, and bats may use sound at high frequencies above human hearing capacity to locate food or to avoid obstacles (Au 1993, Griffin 1959).

Biological sounds have plastic characteristics. They are the life traits that can be modified early by learned and/or culturally transmitted adaptive processes (Kroodsma 2004, Derryberry et al. 2016, Sebastian-Gonzalez & Hart 2017). Quality and amount of sound are sensitive to environmental conditions and interferences (e.g. reverberation, signal attenuation, scattering) due to vegetation or to ground aspect and morphology, and may have a major impact on the effectiveness of this semiotic tool (e.g. Embleton 1963, Eyring 1946).

In some habitats where the visual cues become inefficient, as in dense forests or in deep waters, sounds become the prevalent vehicle of communication and navigation.

The role of sound in human communication is fundamental for the articulation of language, but also for creating cognitive pleasure (e.g. music). In particular, environmental sounds contribute to establishing the sense of place for humans, to reinforcing cultural heritage, and finally to assuring spiritual well-being (Cain et al. 2013, Moscoso et al. 2018).

9.2 Noise

When unwanted, too intense, or too continuous, as with urban technophonies, sound is considered to be noise, at least according to a human perspective. Noise has low intrinsic information and degrades acoustic communication.

Human intrusion has created new conditions in the majority of environments world wide, producing changes in landscapes, and chemical pollution of waters, air, and soils. But the intensive use of mechanical devices (cars, trains, airplanes, boats, industrial machineries, etc.) from urban areas has reached the most remote areas and oceans, creating a further source of "sneaky" acoustic (noise) pollution that produces negative effects on many species, populations, and communities (Luther & Gentry 2013).

Noise may have serious consequences for the acoustic performance of soniferous species, masking their vocalizations and interrupting the communication between individuals (Barber et al. 2010, Curry et al. 2018). It is difficult to manage anthropogenic noise, especially in proximity to great logistic hubs like airports, railway stations, and harbors.

The investigation of the ecological role of sounds is crucial for a complete semiotic landscape investigation. Managing sounds is necessary to reduce, remediate, and improve the quality of habitats for a large assemblage of species.

9.3 A Contribution to Ecoacoustics Epistemology

Recently sound has been recognized as an important component in the ecology of species, favored by the birth of ecoacoustics as a new discipline (Farina 2014, Sueur & Farina 2015, Farina & Gage 2017). Ecoacoustics directly confronts the need to quantify the acoustic energy that flows across the environment, attempting to identify sources and to assess the effects on animal species and their aggregations.

This discipline has been organized on the robust basis of physical acoustics and bioacoustics, and recently according to a relevant epistemology (Farina 2018a) that attributes acoustic phenomenology to adaptive, geographical, behavioral, and ecosemiotic domains.

9.3.1 The Adaptive Domain

The adaptive domain belongs to two main hypotheses: the adaptation hypothesis and the acoustic partitioning hypothesis. The first hypothesis assumes that habitat characteristics influence the acoustic emissions of organisms developed over evolutionary time (Morton 1975, Marten & Marler 1977, Brown & Handford 2000). For example, low frequency songs are used by species in dense forests. It is well-known that low frequency has only minor degradation under these conditions. At the same time, high frequencies are preferred in open habitats where there are not obstacles to the diffusion of acoustic energy.

The acoustic partitioning hypothesis describes the strategy used to avoid the overlap of sounds from different species, thus reducing confusion of messages and interference. This hypothesis is particularly applicable in tropical areas where an amazing diversity of soniferous species, mainly insects and frogs, requires a fine partitioning of frequencies (Lemon et al. 1981, Krause 1993, 2012).

9.3.2 The Geographical Domain

The geographical domain is relevant when acoustic phenomena are investigated at the scale of landscape (Farina 2014). Emerging from the landscape are sounds that result from overlapping, different acoustic sources. The differing contributions of geophonies, biophonies, and technophonies create the soundscape (Pijanowski et al. 2011a) (Figure 14). However, because the landscape is not homogeneous, this is reflected in the soundscape in which there are continuous variations in the percentages of geophonies, biophonies, and technophonies (when present). Thus it is reasonable to admit that these categories of sounds are patchily distributed, like distinct (acoustic) patches or sonotopes (Farina 2014, p. 18). The sonotope is a model conceptually close to the ecotope model in

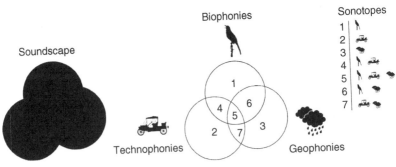

Figure 14 – A soundscape is an important component of a landscape, created by different overlap of geophonies, biophonies, and technophonies. According to the relative dominance of these three components, a soundscape is distinguished by acoustic patches or sonotopes. Here seven types of sonotopes are the results of the overlap between the three components.

landscape ecology. In the same way, every piece of landscape can be classified according to the typology of sonotope present. The unequal distribution of biophonies, when they are the only components of a soundscape, creates an acoustic mosaic of what are called soundtopes (Farina 2014, p. 19). Sonotones are the acoustic margins between soundtopes where species can perceive a different combination of sounds. This effect can create an increase of acoustic uncertainty favored by a causal encounter of different acoustic communities. Sound diversity has been proved to be effected by these factors (Sebastian-Gonzalez & Hart 2017).

The soundscape for the intrinsic properties of sound that are modified by environmental features in a landscape for propagation of acoustic energy and for heterogeneous distribution of soniferous species, has a more fine-grained structure of geographical or vegetation-based descriptors. For example, recently Farina (2019) found distinct sonotopes with an acoustic extension restricted to fifteen meters of radius in a rural landscape. For this reason soundscape is an excellent proxy for landscape complexity, and it represents a novel approach to landscape assessment as well, thanks to a new methodology of acoustic recording that can efficiently collect large data sets without producing an impact on organisms (Sueur 2018).

The spatial heterogeneity of a soundscape formalized by adopting the paradigm of sonotopes can further be associated with a temporal heterogeneity. In this last case we are dealing with a temporary sequence of sounds, in which emergent properties are perceived distinctly and for which it is possible to assign a meaning through an encoding procedure. Such emergent acoustic patterns are called ecoacoustic events by Farina et al. (2016, 2018). Recently it has been demonstrated that ecoacoustic events change according to the temporal scale at which they are detected. To solve the problem of selecting an appropriate temporal scale, a multi-temporal analysis has been proposed, and its interpretation has been assigned to a fractal procedure (Monacchi & Farina 2019, Farina et al. 2020).

9.3.3 The Behavioral Domain

The behavioral domain pertains to the effect of acoustic signals on the behavior of soniferous and non-soniferous species, and on the interactions between species (acoustic communities) and the selection of acoustic habitats.

9.3.3.1 Acoustic Communities

Different species can create temporary acoustic aggregations or acoustic communities (Farina & James 2016). Such communities produce sound by using internal or extra-body sound-producing tools, and occur in aquatic (freshwater and marine) and terrestrial environments. Acoustic communities are characterized by a high dynamic, changing species composition at hourly, daily, and seasonal intervals.

According to a human perspective there are at least three kinds of acoustic communities, based on the frequency of acoustic emissions: (1) infrasonic (e.g. whales (Cetacea) <20 Hz); (2) "ordinary" 20–20,000 Hz (the majority of vertebrates, humans included); and (3) ultra-sonic >20,000 Hz (e.g. bats (*Chiroptera*), dolphins (*Cetacea*) and some insects). An acoustic community is composed of emitters and receivers that in turn reverse their roles. The existence of an acoustic community requires that part of the acoustic sign system of one species can be transferred with meaning to another species. In this way, every species can interact for some extension with the life cycle of another species that shares the same habitat. Some benefits from creating such temporary aggregations of acoustic signals are based on the avoidance of interspecific competition achieved by an active exchange of information on the presence of potential predators, on the location of food sources, and on the availability of nesting places. Influence on individual vocalization is evident in some species of birds that mimic songs and calls of other species living in the same habitat. For example, among birds, the European robin (*Erithacus rube-cula*) and jay (*Garrulus glandarius*) have the capacity to mimic many species with which they come in contact. Ethological understanding of this behavior remains largely obscure, although it is reasonable to imagine some benefits.

9.3.3.2 Acoustic Habitats

The selection of habitat is an obligatory activity for every species and is represented by a multiplicity of decisions made on the basis of the physical and biological characters of the environment. An acoustic habitat is defined as a space selected by a species according to a unique emergent sonic ambient character perceived as favorable (Mullet et al. 2017). Evidence from field observations indicates that species utilize the acoustic information in the environment to select places in which to establish breeding or foraging territory (e.g. Blumenrath & Dabelsteen 2004, Derryberry 2009, Both & Grant 2012). For instance the black-throated blue warbler (*Dendroica caerulescens*) prefers low-quality habitats in which conspecific calls were played back, to more favorable habitats (Betts et al. 2008), and Chaffinches (*Fringilla coelebs*) and willow warblers (*Phylloscopus trochilus*) were observed at higher density in areas where resident tits (*Parus* sp.) were present in abundance (Mönkkönen et al. 1990).

The acoustic quality of habitats coincides with an increase in the survival of species. Some species are very sensitive to this quality and in worse conditions, such as a very noisy urban environment or one close to highly trafficked roads, may be replaced by less sensitive species (Francis et al. 2009, Shannon et al. 2014). Recent evidence indicates that blackcap (*Sylvia atricapilla*), a small songbird very common in European shrubland, has a subordinate behavior (to stop singing) when the red-billed leiothrix (*Leiothrix lutea*), a recent invasive species in southern Europe, is singing (Farina et al. 2013.) Because of this behavior, it is reasonable to suspect a strong competition between the two species in terms of common habitat and food. In such cases, blackcap abundance declines locally and is substituted by populations of red-billed leiothrix.

9.3.4 The Ecosemiotic Domain

The ecosemiotic domain pertains to the acoustic codes used to transmit intra- and interspecific information between individuals, populations, and communities and the acoustic mechanisms (acoustic eco-fields) used by individual species to track resources such as refuges, food, nesting places, etc.

References to codes are not used as much in ecology as they are in genetics (Mislan 2016), but their fundamental qualities are well-defined "as mechanisms that establish an arbitrary set of connections between two or more components (organisms and/or their aggregations) of a complex system" (Farina & Pieretti 2014). In intra- and interspecific communication the movement of information from an emitter to a receiver is obtained by encoding and decoding processes.

During the decoding process, information on habitat suitability, presence of predators, location of food sources, and availability and location of refuges is sent from a transmitter to a receiver. Several species are able to interpret to some extent the acoustic signals of other species (Alatalo et al. 1985, Magrath et al. 2015, Fallow & Magrath 2010, Dorado-Correa et al. 2013, Wheatcroft & Price 2015). Evidence was collected through behavioral investigation; when it was transferred into a spatial context, it created the conditions for the introduction of the acoustic eco-field model.

The acoustic eco-field is employed by species to track specific resources, using configurations of acoustic signals to which specific meanings have been assigned. This model was developed on the assumption that biophonies and ecoacoustic events in general are carriers of some type of relevant information. For example, flocks of starlings (*Sturnus vulgaris*) at roosting assemblages actively exchange acoustic information on location and abundance of food (Ward & Zahavi, 1973). Acoustic spatiality, origin, and position of an acoustic signal, compared with signals emitted in other positions and circumstances, represent relevant information used by individuals during acoustic eco-field procedures.

We recognize the difficulty of describing ecoacoustic processes, because they are the expression of mobile organisms, they are emitted for a short period of time, and they have a high variability in their structure. Nevertheless, the amount of information associated with this structured energy is very high. A sound is appreciated for a very short period of time, and when it is analyzed, it is possible to see what patterns are present at different temporal resolutions. For instance, the song of a bird shows patterns on a scale from a millisecond to minutes in length. The open question of what better temporal resolution could be used to extract information from a song, is a question without a univocal reply.

There are other open questions when sound is considered from an ecosemiotic perspective. For example, what is the amount of acoustic energy emitted that can make the difference in terms of quality and meaning of a message?

9.3.4.1 Near and Far Field

Sound rapidly degrades in space (Naguib & Wiley 2001), and the discrimination of sounds from a near or a far field is a way to try to model this characteristic, where near and far fields are, respectively, short distances or large distances from the place of detection.

The near and the far field have different extensions according to the reference species, and the two fields remain important models for understanding the complex replies that species exhibit. When a receiver is inside the near field of an emitter, the signal that it receives is strong because not degraded by distance. We know that sound energy radiating from a source decreases in proportion of $1/r^2$, where r is the distance between emitter and receiver. When the receiver operates in the far-field mode, on the other hand, the sound is perceived as degraded, because it has lost a portion of its information. The encoding and decoding procedures are both sensitive to the distance at which different acoustic codes are generated. It is important to understand that an acoustic signal has a meaning according to the emitting and hearing contexts in which such a signal is embedded. A sound leaves the emitter in a "naked" status and wears "clothes" of meaning along the way until its complete degradation and disuse.

The interpretation of ecoacoustic events defined as a sequence of acoustic patterns for which every species assigns meanings, is the required step toward a better comprehension of the semiotic complexity of soundscapes.

Information transmitted during an ecoacoustic event can be measured to some extent before a meaning is attributed to it. For instance, the alarm call of a tit in the presence of a cat can be measured in terms of intensity, frequency of repetition, and length of repetition, independently of its classification as an alarm call. This quantification is possible thanks to the novel metrics developed by ecoacoustics scholars during recent decades (e.g. Sueur et al. 2014, Sueur 2018) and based on the transposition of acoustic waves from the temporal domain into a frequential one obtained using the Fourier transform algorithms (Fourier 1822).

Between the different indices tested and used in different terrestrial and aquatic contexts we use the Acoustic Complexity Indices (ACI) (Pieretti et al. 2011). This index, elaborated for the first time by Farina and Morri (2008), was conceived in order to produce a direct and quick quantification of animal vocalizations by processing the intensities of audio files. The ACI formula is based on the observation that many biotic sounds, such as bird songs, are characterized by an intrinsic variability of intensities. Measuring the differences of intensities along an appropriate temporal interval, ACI measures the amount of information present in that signal. Moreover the signal has an internal complexity that sends more information through. Generally technophonies have a more homogeneous internal structure, and this produces low values in ACI. The great sensitivity of ACI to the complexity of acoustic signals is confirmed by several investigations carried out in different environments (e.g. Farina et al. 2011, Towsey et al. 2018).

The extension of the soundscape concept to perception and cognition of animals represents a true challenge because little is known about the listening and interpretive capacity of soniferous species. To overcome such difficulties, the Ecoacoustic Event Detection and Identification procedure (EEDI) is proposed as a statistical method for assigning a specific code algorithmically to an aggregate sequence of sounds (Figure 15). This procedure my be powered by the application of a further fractal analysis (Hsü 1993, Bigerelle & Iost 2000, Monacchi & Farina 2019) to better illustrate the complexity of the acoustic system.

9.4 Concluding Remarks

The acoustic component of the landscape plays a fundamental role in the overall ecosemiosis of humans as well as animals. Sounds contribute to maintaining a strict connection between people and environment. In fact, sounds are extensively used not only in intraspecific communication, but also to assure interspecific connections, facilitating important exchanges of information. Sounds are transmitted in every medium and are not affected by some sources of energy such as sunlight. For this reason, sounds are often used in environmental conditions where visual cues are ineffective, as in deep waters or in dense forest covers. Humans require a "noisy" world, where in this case noise is not a negative

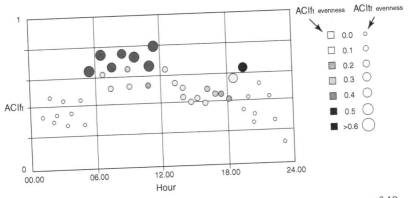

Figure 15 – Representation, in a Euclidean ecoacoustic event space, of 40 hypothetical ecoacoustic events. Each circle represents the $ACIf_t$ evenness value (y-axis) for a given hour of day (x-axis). The dimension of the circle represents $ACIf_t$ classes that range from 0 to 1. The shades of grey represent the classes of $ACIf_t$ evenness.

attribute of the environment but a necessary source of information. In Rachel Carson's important book, Silent Spring (Carson 1962), the silence of nature was for the first time related to an indiscriminate and massive use of pesticides that had facilitated organism extinction. The silence in nature is not a poetic metaphor but is instead a real symptom of some misfunctioning of ecosystems. Sounds from physical phenomena like falling rain and blowing wind have a relatively homogeneous inner structure with few frequential and intensity variations, but they are highly unpredictable in time. The occurrence of rain, for instance, does not have a temporal or spatial regularity, but its acoustic footprint is distinctive. On the other hand, sounds of biological origin generally have a very complex and in some cases irregular internal structure, but their occurrence is highly predictable. For example, choruses of birds occur at dawn and dusk during the breeding season and are regulated by the availability of light. The singing activity of birds is regulated by seasons and by the length of the day. Organisms invest a lot of energy in acoustic emissions, and we expect advantages in the economy of nature.

Soundscape and its components (sonotopes, soundtopes, and sonotones) provide substantial information about the structure and functioning of landscape and represent one of the most important sources of meaning for every category of people, from scientists to visitors, contributing to human well-being to an equal or greater degree than visual cues.

10 Cultural Landscapes

10.1 Synthesis

Cultural landscapes are the reservoir of ecosemiosis required to interpret a rich collection of signals that are the product of natural and cultural processes stratified in time and integrated in space. Rural sanctuaries are examples of a modern interpretation of cultural landscape finalized for biological conservation in respect to sustainable economic development.

Nature can be seen in the majority of terrestrial areas as a human artifact. The semethic relationship between humans and other organisms is central to this formation in many global regions in human-coupled ecosystems spatially portrayed by landscapes.

A cultural landscape is one in which patterns and processes are the result of a long period of human interference on compatible terms with natural dynamics. For example, in Australia, aboriginal people have shaped the landscape with 47,000 years of burning. The same strategy has been used by Native Americans for a very long time up until the European colonial period (Stewart 2002, Vale 2002). Such intervention has modified the structure and dynamics of entire land mosaics, affecting distribution and abundance of plants and animals. Every historical epoch has had consequences on landscapes. Human pressure on landscape is in relation to human dynamics, so that when people abandon some areas, such as along the Italian coastal swamps, these areas evolve for the effect of a secondary succession that shapes the landscape and recreates a wilderness over time. A cultural landscape, in a human perspective, may exist at different levels of naturalness, offering additional sources of inspiration, beliefs, identity, and belonging.

Cultural landscapes are full of signals, symbols, and signs resulting from an intense elaboration of physical reality and feeling. In rural communities every place has a specific name that indicates past ownership (e.g. field of Anthony), or the character of the soil surface (e.g. "Lama" to indicate a steep soil), or the appearance of soil (e.g. "Black Hills"), or the level of fertility (e.g. "Badlands"). For this reason the ecosemiotic approach to the interpretation of a cultural landscape requires a more advanced cultural approach. The use of maps to describe this landscape enables people to navigate between physical and cognitive objects. In contrast, the ecosemiosis of a natural landscape is apparently less complex, at least in terms of extractable information. For instance, most people cannot distinguish in detail the hundreds of individual species singing in a tropical forest at the same time and in a narrow spatial range.

The description of a cultural landscape is a complex process requiring competencies from differing and distant disciplines ranging from geography, to anthropology, archaeology, art history, economy, geology, botany, zoology, animal behavior, ecology, cognitive ecology, ecosemiotics, and many more.

10.2 The "Empty" and "Full" World Models

Two different models by which humanity interprets our relationship with nature have been recently discussed (Farina et al. 2003). The "empty world model" states that some intact remnants of nature must be created and maintained for future generations, far from human influence. However, outside these areas, development is tolerated for the production of goods and services. The "full world model" recognizes the presence of humanity everywhere, with a growing impact on the entire Earth system. According to the latter model, it is essential to preserve natural processes also in areas considered at a low level of naturalness, such as urban parks, farmlands, managed forests, and lagoons. Improving natural processes should represent part of a global strategy for preserving ecosystems, their structures, and their dynamics. The full world model in part coincides with the cultural landscape conceptualization defined by geographic areas in which the relationships between human activity and environment have created ecological, socio-economic, and cultural patterns and feedback mechanisms that govern the presence, distribution, and abundance of species assemblages.

10.3 The Characteristics of Cultural Landscapes

A cultural landscape is a complex ecosystem in its own right in which some properties emerge beyond the sum of its parts. It differs from a natural landscape because of visible or invisible human actions. Such a landscape is the result of strict relationships between human actions for the extraction of resources in a sustainable way, using best knowledge and experience, and receiving tremendous feedback that in the long term has influenced the strategies of human societies. Highly urbanized areas and areas that have been transformed by agriculture and forestry in a short period of time are excluded from this category of landscapes. In fact, landscapes modified unintentionally by human impacts cannot be considered cultural landscapes, and they often present complicated structures that require constant stewardship to be maintained.

For instance, the development of transportation infrastructures like roads, railways, and sewage plants often fragments habitats and modifies the underground and surficial water circulation, increasing impervious surfaces and creating barriers to animal movements. All these infrastructures impact on the ecosystems at a multiplicity of scales producing deep changes in the ecological processes.

A cultural landscape is composed of physical objects spatially arranged that create a "material cultural landscape," and by spiritual and symbolic objects that create an "immaterial cultural landscape."

The manipulation of nature is often considered an impacting process, whereas a natural landscape is seen as worthy of preservation in any way. But this is only part of the story, because a cultural landscape can create a mix of interactions between artifacts and nature that increases some ecological processes that work together to maintain or develop biodiversity. In this sense, humans are like keystone species that shape the landscape, enabling the coexistence of culture and nature. Today, cultural landscapes are often assigned a low rank in the political agenda and are often considered "lands of conquest" in which urban and industrial settlements and logistic infrastructures can be expanded.

Too often human development is associated with the reduction and degradation of biodiversity. If this is true in tropical regions, other regions of the world that have been modified for very long historical periods by human intervention are still reservoirs of biodiversity. This is the case for the Mediterranean basin, affected by human-induced changes since the glaciers receded at the end of the last Ice Age (Di Castri 1981, Blondel & Aronson 1999, Blondel 2006), during which time plant and animal domestication has favored several species.

In these regions human intervention by a moderate disturbance regime (fire, grazing, plowing, periodical pruning) has modified soil structure and seasonal cycles of nutrients, affecting plant distribution and animal migration and dynamics, and enabling the conservation of a great number of species (Naveh 1974, 1994, Grove & Rackham 2001). The cause of persisting biodiversity in such regions when compared to regions like northern America offers interesting elements for discussion about the effects of human impact on the environment. Human disturbance on land cover may represent a surrogate for the intermediate level of disturbance of ecosystems, according to a diversity-disturbance hypothesis celebrated by the ecology (Grime 1973).

The separation between a human world and "natural" world has dominated the debate for centuries, from Greek rationalism (Abram 2012), to Judeo-Christian tradition (White 1967), to current impassioned debates within the scientific and humanities communities (e.g. Jenkins 2002).

Cultural landscape apparently is perceived differently by scientific disciplines from the way it is seen in the humanities (Plumwood 2006). In the former, a cultural landscape is a modification of physical and biological entities operated by humans according to procedures that should assure a long-term sustainability to populations. For the humanities, a cultural landscape is not only a mental construct, often supported by myths (Tilley 1994) in which historical events are fixed in a perennial memory, but also a place where the active role of indigenous people becomes central to perpetuate some successful adaptations (Sauer 1925, Plumwood 2006).

Archeology, anthropology, human geography, and environmental phyloso-phy are some branches of humanities that recognize the central position of landscape in the development of human models from individuals to complex multiethnic societies.

In particular the philosopher Gary Backhaus (2006) has presented an interesting synthesis based on the new concept of "ecoscape." For this author, "ecoscape is a spatial configuration of relations and interrelations of life-sustaining world... Ecoscapes are the spatial configurations of ecosystems."

Wang et al. (2010) define an ecoscape as "a multidimensional landscape of a social-economic-natural complex ecosystem, combining geographical pat-terns, hydrological process, biological vitality, anthropological dynamics, and aesthetic contexts."

This neologism represents a good example of integration between humanities and natural sciences, although it appears sporadically in the ecological literature.

For instance, Lidicker (2008) proposed this term as a substitute for ecosystem with its superior level of organization after individuals, populations. and com-munities. Recently Farina and James (in prep.) have revised the ecoscape concept introducing the new term "vivoscape" as the field of existence or domain of species representing the totality of biological, ecological, and semi-otical relationships between an organism and its operational environment.

According to these authors, a vivoscape is the domain of relationships between a taxon and its environment and is composed of (sensorial and rela-tional) communication channels with different flow intensity and direction (toward the taxon master, from the master, and to abiotic agencies [mineral soil, air, water] and to other related taxa). This model seems appropriate for its spatial competencies as "function-circle"(Uexküll 1926) of individual species (taxon) and can be considered the functional application of the ecological niche concept (Patten & Auble 1981).

Different groups of people interpret the same landscape differently because of varying needs and aspirations that characterize their perceptual exploration of the surroundings. The values they extract from a landscape change according to culture, sub-culture, region, and time. We only need to mention tourists and residents, whose visions of their surroundings are completely divergent. As reported by Jones (1991), "A natural landscape for Norwegians may be a cultural landscape for Sami."

In the reality, non-human (natural) and human (cultural) agencies are both operating shaping landscapes.

10.4 Ontogenesis of a Cultural Landscape

Human history and ecosystem processes are the two main "agents" of the ontogenesis of a cultural landscape. The human skill in the use of natural resources, accumulated along the course of human history and resulting from a deep knowledge of natural processes, has created strict relationships with several human-tolerant organisms. The fine resolution with which soils have been cultivated and the creation of specific ecotopes according to local characteristics of geography, soil, and micro-climate have favored the distribution and persistence of particular species of wild plants and animals. These plants and animals are favored by human cyclical plowing, and in general by the stewardship of pastures, woodlands, and marshes (Figure 16). For instance, several bird species most menaced by the change of land use, such as occupation of rural spaces by industries, have elected rural areas as habitats. Particular important results affect the relationship between domestic and wild animals. For instance, the Camargue area at the mouth of the Rhone River in southern France is a major area for wintering birds, but it would not be so important without the presence of a special cultivation of marshes, fields, and riparian woodland plantations where horses and bulls are keystone species that play the same role as the wild ungulates in the African savannah or bison on North American prairies. Similarly, although to a lesser extent, the "Italian Maremma" at the border between the Lazio and Tuscany regions is strategic for overwintering by

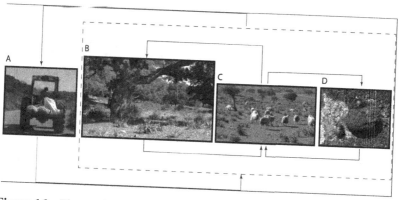

Figure 16 – The rural system of Sardinia Island (Italy) where the key species is represented by the shepherd (A). Sheep rearing modifies the agro-ecosystem favoring a land cover dominated by cork oaks (*Quercus suber*) (B) and by grazed prairies (C). Sheep have a great influence on the cork oaks and on invertebrate fauna (dung beetles) (D).

many birds attracted to the abundance of resources made available by the grazing regime of semi-wild cows and horses.

Managing fire, a practice initiated by hunter-gatherers from at least 500,000 years ago, probably initiated the development of grazing and browsing areas for domestic ruminants (Naveh 1974). The domestication of plants and animals since 10,000 years ago in the Fertile Crescent (Breasted 1905) – modern day Iraq, Israel and Palestinian territories, Syria, Lebanon, Egypt, Jordan, and the southeastern fringes of Turkey – has caused the diffusion from this region of at least 500 cultivated species and varieties of plants (Miller 1992). Water management has been a key process in the Mediterranean domestication process. Water utilized for irrigation, and engineering infrastructures for regulating natural floods and to increase the self-fertilization of soils, have changed soil pedogenesis to favor cultivated plants. Modification of the slope of hills and low mountains by a system of terraces has been a further relevant manipulation of the Mediterranean region, still present in today's landscape from Greece to Italy, Spain, and islands across all the Mediterranean (Lepart & Debusse 1992). Terraces are also present in many other regions such as Southeast Asia and Central and South America.

The agricultural systems that have shaped the Mediterranean landscape in the past were based on the Roman system sylva-saltus-ager (woodland, pasture, field), in which each treatment was separated by the others, creating a mosaic of ecotopes (Figure 17). But other systems compete for richness and diversity of life forms in the Mediterranean. We refer to the Dehesa-Montado

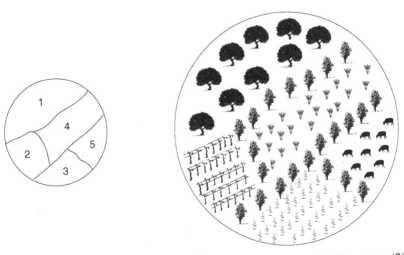

Figure 17 – Schematic example of Mediterranean ecotopes. (1) Olive trees, (2) Vineyard, (3) Maize field, (4) Wheat field, (5) Pastures.

(Spain-Portugal) system where the three Roman practices were combined in a unique system.

The role of grazing by domestic livestock and wild ungulates is relevant. Evidence shows a higher diversity of plants on islands overgrazed by the Cretan wild goat (*Capra aegagrus cretica*) than in another ungrazed island (Papageorgiou 1979).

Knowledge, experience, and interactions are the basis of the human fortune in shaping landscapes. Landscapes are the connection between human needs and actions and ecosystems and their collection of living forms. This accumulated and stratified knowledge of the function of natural and modified systems is today at risk of exclusion from our cultural heritage, thus triggering a further and deeper planetary environmental crisis.

10.5 Values from a Cultural Landscape

Romantic literature and painting have greatly contributed to the myth of the cultural landscape that in turn has sustained and developed the modern industry of mass tourism. Tourism has a special vision of the landscape that searches for beauty, with a preference for visual elements and photography, neglecting everyday landscapes simply perceived as a source of goods and services. The touristic perception of a landscape can transform a cultural landscape into an object of "touristic" contemplation. The Cinque Terre region in northern Italy is an example of a cultural landscape that has assumed the role of tourist destination of global importance: terraced vineyards and seaside villages actually like a postcard attract a million foreign visitors each year.

According to the cultural model utilized, three basic visions may be drawn from a cultural landscape. In a first approach the landscape is a collection of physical objects that can be investigated using mainly geographic disciplines. A second approach considers the landscape as a collection of valuable elements like monuments, historical buildings, rare natural phenomena, etc., where functional values seem to prevail over aesthetic elements. Finally in a third approach a landscape is a mental construction as in the example of Australian aboriginal people, and the way it is perceived depends on individual feeling, culture, and skill. According to concluding comments from Tilley (1994: 67), landscape is a part of mythopoesis, peopled by ancestral and spiritual entities. The presentation of myths creates a spiritual landscape in which natural systems are the result of an ancestral intent in which hunter-gatherers or subsistence cultivators were linked with nature by complex mechanisms and tradeoffs. According to this perspective the landscape is the realization of a dream and not the interpretation of ecological reality. However, the origin of myth is a way to explain the complexity of the environment based not on a scientific neutrality but rather on human meta-phorical representation.

10.6 Conservation

A cultural landscape has been recognized by UNESCO and IUCN as an area in which human history and the continuity of lives and activities are worthy of preservation (van Droste et al. 1995). To preserve a cultural landscape means to maintain the historical processes of interaction and reciprocal influence between people and nature. To achieve this, it is not possible to maintain a cultural landscape as it was centuries or millennia ago, but rather a methodology of management must be applied that guarantees goods and services for a dynamic society, assuring a resilient evolution in this way. In the past, natural constraints had limited and regulated human action, but today these barriers can easily be surpassed by supplying energy and technologies. Legal regulations can prevent this kind of disruption of a cultural landscape.

The concept of cultural landscapes is quite popular in the humanities, where a dualistic representation of reality poses humanities versus science (Plumwood 2006). Cultural landscapes stress the role of indigenous people's cultural agency prior to the colonial era in which European colonists wrongly believed that landscapes were shaped only by nonhuman (natural) agencies. But according to Sauer (1925), "Culture is the agent, the natural area is the medium, the cultural landscape is the result." The term culture must be associated with the learned form of adaptation that is present in both humans and other animals.

However, both cultural heritage and natural heritage are the components of a cultural landscape where the agency that should receive priority in conserva-tion policies is the natural one. Without natural processes, it is not possible for a cultural agent to act. The agencies involved in the cultural landscape are necessarily collaborative.

In North America, Australia, and tropical South America, the idea of undis-turbed nature pre-colonial settlement is a false paradigm to be rejected. Wilderness is a concept that ignores completely the role of indigenous people. Conserving a cultural landscape is not a simple matter. In fact, conservation may represent a paradox for a cultural landscape that is the result of long-term, successive, and stratified adaptive changes. But as in urban areas, "renewal" means the erasure of some ordinary buildings but the preservation of monu-ments, churches, and historical buildings. At the same time, conserving a cultural landscape means the preservation of at least the memory of key elements that are the foundation of a framework of symbols.

To try to decide if it would be better conserving or changing, it would be useful to argue that in a cultural landscape people extract resources in sustainable ways, and the effect of these procedures shapes the landscape. The point is that the so-called "traditional practices" are intended simply to manage resources in a sustainable way, that are in turn indispensable elements of a cultural landscape.

10.7 Strategies for Implementing the Environmental Humanities Approach: The Rural Sanctuary, a Simple Model for Reconciling Nature and People

Today most people live in great urban and metropolitan areas (UNFPA 2020; Reba et al. 2016). Jobs or economic independence, healthy conditions, and access to recreational facilities are the key goals of satisfactory life, at least in modern and developed societies. The reconciliation of people and nature today requires an intense process of education, because the primeval adaptive forces that in the past created strong linkages between the different anthropological models and natural processes quickly disappeared as a consequence of industrialization associated with new social/economic/cultural habits. In Western countries, culture that for a very long time enabled the creation of a strict relationship between people and natural processes has disappeared within a few generations. Today people are facing real problems in understanding how to maintain the health of ecosystems on which human life still fully depends. This story is a little different in poor areas of the Earth, where food, security, democracy, and human rights are primary needs to be achieved. In both cases nature and its values are on the sidelines, but for different reasons. In the case of well-off societies, nature is associated with recreation and tourism. Nature is considered to be a place in which to spend holidays and to consume without limits. In the case of "undeveloped" countries, where basic daily human needs are not being met, however, nature is the source of further difficulties; areas uncontrolled, from a security point of view, are sources of higher risk of natural events like hurricanes, floods, landslides, volcanic eruptions, and tsunamis, and where recovery becomes slow and difficult, when compared to wealthy urban societies. Moreover, nature is considered a source of pest organisms that can compete for crops in tropical regions (e.g. orangutans or elephants that are considered symbolic animals in Western culture, but are perceived as a calamity in some tropical regions, at least in these recent years where deforestation and agriculture intensification have reduced habitat for these animals).

The paradigm of nature conservation solves only in part the problems that people have created, with nature seen as neutral in attitude, disinterested or indifferent. In fact, humanity cannot thrive on this Earth if it ignores the unavoidable impact it is producing on ecosystems. Policies that respect natural processes still struggle to reduce the "physiological" impact on nature due to the great numbers of humans in every part of the world.

It is important to understand that in areas where human density is high, people must take active care of natural processes to reduce their impact. This fact is often neglected by conservation measures. Unfortunately the spread of wildfires in high density settlements such as in California is of growing concern. There is much evidence that people cannot retain a neutral attitude toward nature. In areas where water deficit increases the risk of wildfires, it is not possible to facilitate the growth of shrublands and trees, hoping for good luck. It is not by chance that across the Mediterranean in the present times, landscapes persist that are structured as open savanna. Historical deforestation dating back to the Holocene, and a landscape designed according to resilient assets, require the action of people whose goal is making primary resources available for people, according to the keystone role of humans. Conservation of an integral nature remains an activity restricted to small areas neglected because of remoteness or historical difficulties of extracting resources (Kopnina 2016).

We are aware that the structure of a landscape is the result of a succession of historical events that have modified the use of land, affecting the distribution of natural vegetation and associated animal communities. At the same time, the influence of political and social dynamics continuously produces new spatial configurations in which cultivation, urban logistical infrastructures, and protected areas are dynamically rearranged. Thus it is impossible without a robust ecological model to design a landscape ex-novo, as it would be designed in a recreational park for an urban area. Despite these difficulties, recently we have proposed the "rural sanctuary" as a model of interaction between people and nature, where human action consists in the production of resources and at the same time offers opportunities for a great number of adaptive organisms to receive benefits (Farina 2018b).

The term sanctuary, from Latin "sanctus" or holy, is defined as " a religious place where exceptional spiritual and supernatural events have been observed and celebrated, and buildings and monuments have been erected (Treccani 2020.)" (Farina 2018b). This term has been used in nature conservation as a synonym for wildlife refuge to indicate a place of protection for rare and endangered species. According to an ecosemiotic perspective, a rural sanctuary is a rural area in which traditional farm practices offer refuge, food, and reproductive opportunities to a large collection of species. Rural sanctuaries are an application of the "full world model" that are small pieces of land in which people produce crops with the strategy of respecting and preserving natural processes, offering accidentally the resources for plant and animal communities (Farina et al. 2003). The substantial difference between a rural sanctuary and a wildlife refuge, or other types of nature protection, consists in the strict relationship between human activity and nature conservation. In particular, farming activity adopted in a rural sanctuary is inspired by traditional farming and excludes intensive market farming. The main goal of a rural sanctuary is not to protect a particular species but to "involuntarily" create new habitats for species attracted by resources that are the byproduct of traditional farming. The landowner does not receive subsidies, because these actions are voluntary.

A rural sanctuary is not a source of social conflicts because traditional farming is perfectly incorporated into the dynamics of society, and its farming practices do not require specific regulation but are recognized and accepted by local human communities. A rural sanctuary is also the source of inspiration, amenities, and a sense of belonging for people. It represents a collection of eco-fields used by people for the extraction of resources, but contemporary with the involuntary design utilized is the source of eco-fields for wild species. A contemporary rural sanctuary is governed by ecosemiotic mechanisms that primarily assure resources to a landowner who, because of a specific cultural attitude, can interpret environmental language. These communication mechanisms are not based on a formal explicit language (sequence of words), but on a sequence of actions. For instance, the periodic mowing of grasses attracts swallows and swifts that find insects on the disturbed grass layer. Farmer and birds create an indirect connection based on actions of friendship, and thus animals can reduce their physical distance from the working farmer. In this way, an exchange of semethic information moves from humans to animals, and vice-versa. The spatial arrangement of cultivated patches can encourage visits from animals in search of food. Alternation between ploughed, mowed, and grazed fields is a real attraction for many organisms. When a farmer organizes their activities in order to attract animals, they implicitly use an efficient nonverbal communication. This can be observed also beyond the rural context. For example, in backyard gardens, if people love birds, they can express this by supplying food and fresh water in dispensers – ecosemiotic tools for saying "I love you."

A rural sanctuary can be understood as a hierarchy of eco-fields designed to track specific resources primarily for human use, and secondarily as a place where species-specific eco-fields are involuntarily created. For instance, some breeding or sanctuary species-specific eco-fields needed by birds are represented by fruit trees planted and nurtured to produce fruits. More diverse is the land-use mosaic inside a rural sanctuary, which provides more possibilities for species to identify favorable habitats. In some cases inside a rural sanctuary true

Figure 18 – The Mediterranean rural landscape offers temporary refuge as a stopover for migrating birds. In this figure a whinchat (*Saxicola rubetra*) finds a favorable temporary habitat in a vineyard where a short-grass layer offers insects that can easily be located. The branches of the grapevine, covered by blossoming buds, are optimal observation points for birds to locate insects on the soil surface. This land configuration is present for a short period that coincides with the whinchat migration (late April-mid-May) in the Western Palearctic. In a few weeks vineyards become dense bush-like groves and attract birds like blackcap (*Sylvia atricapilla*) that usually live in shrublands; meanwhile the whinchats have already established breeding territories in open areas beyond the Alps.

ecological traps are produced (Battin 2004, Hale & Swearer 2017). At the same time, a rural sanctuary may be considered as part of a network of other sanctuaries, and the animal populations inside may respond to the dynamic of metapopulations (Hanski 1999). A rural sanctuary offers a spatial and temporal mosaic of sink and source patches, as well (Pulliam 1988) (Figure 18).

The rural sanctuary model can be associated with every rural landscape around the world, but its definition and characteristics have been designed for the Mediterranean region where rural sanctuaries may preserve relevant areas for biodiversity.

There is evidence that animals have a great sensitivity also to minimal changes in land use, and that the high dynamics with which the sanctuaries are managed create the certainty that several species may find suitable habitats.

From a market economy perspective, rural sanctuaries play a secondary role, but in terms of ecosystem services and consequent benefits, rural sanctuaries offer refuge to a relevant number of rare animals and represent a primary seed bank for plants.

This model does not require specific public regulation but instead is the result of an individual choice to contribute to maintaining the biodiversity in a selected area.

A rural sanctuary is a hot spot for biodiversity and when present in several locations across the landscape may represent an ecological network that can buffer/contrast with the loss of habitats and reduction of species varieties. The rural landscape belongs to the great family of cultural landscapes where biophilia represents a powerful educational tool to be offered in a genuine and direct way to young generations as an example of positive interaction between people and nature.

11 Conclusions

The ecosemiotic paradigm is based on the assumption that a flow of information transformed by encoding/decoding processes in meaning sustains the interactions between organisms and their environment. The landscape plays an important role as common reference for the ecosemiotic spatially explicit domain for all the organisms that operate according to complex sensorial mechanisms, where spatiality and heterogeneity reflect distribution and availability of the resources that are the fuel necessary for maintaining living systems. The landscape is a depositary for a plethora of signification processes originating from patterns such as the dimension of mosaic components, patch size and shape, mosaic heterogeneity, ecotones, and spatial patch arrangement; and by processes like disturbance, fragmentation, and connectivity. Complexity, uncertainty, information, and resources heterogeneously distributed in landscapes are the major ingredients that in varying degrees are certified, captured, and interpreted through organisms' ecosemiotic processes.

Mechanisms of perception and successive cognitive elaborations guarantee permanent contacts and interactions between organisms and their surroundings. Every organism releases signals that may become signs for other individuals and species, and in turn interprets using a signification process for signals from the external abiotic and biotic world. These signals, when converted into signs by decoding procedures, are utilized by species to reduce environmental uncertainty and to increase confidence with individual Umwelten. The majority of ecosemiotic relationships are statistically improbable, but mastered by encoding/decoding procedures, and consequently contain high probabilistic information that progressively, during the process of signification, is transformed into semantic information. This produces conditions for the establishment of complex relationships between organisms and between organism and environment that may present high redundancy, which in turn favors environmental stability.

Genetic and cultural ignorance about what happens all around represent major obstacles for the reduction of environmental uncertainty. However, on the other hand, ignorance that is the result of biological and ecological isolation or incapacity to extract further information from the Latent Landscape, is necessary to reduce the effects of interspecies competition that occurs when the same resources are shared by different species. We acknowledge the paradox that ecological isolation (a narrow ecological niche, when an ecological paradigm is adopted) produces negative effects from one side yet positive ones from another. In fact, ignorance contributes to the reduction of the interception of environmental signals that, when too numerous, can affect the functionality of the entire system stressed by high energetic costs paid to decipher an overabundant flow of information. At the same time, ignorance has negative effects when it prevents the discovery of new adaptive mechanisms with a consequent over-exposure of individuals to environmental risks produced by unexpected events like predation, food shortage, and climatic stress. A tradeoff between ignorance and ecosemiotic knowledge balances these opposite effects.

The pairing of ecological and ecosemiotic paradigms has been demonstrated to be extremely fruitful in terms of comprehension of natural phenomena and human processes, in the attempt to bring humans to an understanding of greater closeness. It appears to be a reliable approach to explore the species-to-species and species-to-environment ecosemiotic relationships, because the common currency exchanged is represented by quantifiable and statistically manageable information.

Ecosemiotics opens new possibilities for describing and understanding the complexity of the environment, increasingly menaced by a growing human impact. The "impoverishment" of complexity increases the risk of species extinction, simplification and shortening of food webs, loss of genetic diversity, and rarefaction of species.

The majority of ecological paradigms, theories, and models can be interpreted with the adoption of the ecosemiotics approach. Emblematic is the example of noise in ecoacoustic investigations. Noise is an unwanted sound for humans and many animals, with species-specific thresholds of tolerance.

From an ecological perspective noise masks other sounds, reducing the possibility for an individual species to adequately scan the environment. From an ecosemiotic perspective, noise that simply represents information at which decoding processes can't attribute a meaning saturates communication channels preventing species-to-species interactions. The two hypotheses are not in contradiction with each other but develop two separate narratives and evidences. In ecology, the effect of noise is measurable in terms of animal displacement, reduction of reproductive success, and reduction in communication display. In ecosemiotics noise is a quantity of energy that impedes communication in some extension. This energy can be measured, and its quality can be translated by an encoding process and labeling. The Ecoacoustic Event Detection and Identification procedure (EEDI) (see Section 9) is an example of this process that aggregates and categorizes acoustic data as ecoacoustic events that are assigned specific codes. Finally, a multiscalar analysis explores the behavior of the system at different temporal resolutions by a fractal analysis. This statistical approach represents a first attempt to manage information produced by ecosemiotic processes.

Landscape ecosemiotics enables us to decipher the abiotic and biotic signals that emerge from the landscape, and to quantify the flow of information activated by individual species perception. This quantification is of primary importance for evaluating the level of resilience and fragility of systems, and the rate of changes occurring in a landscape for the combined effects of ecological succession, land use dynamics, climate change, and the turnover of human policies.

Moreover, landscape ecosemiotics offers a powerful observatory to the humanities for penetrating the secrets of the environment and thus gaining knowledge of the function of the human mind, seizing a great opportunity for deciphering ecological and biological codes.

The reconciliation of the humanities and natural sciences is urgent for the preservation of human and natural heritages with a spirit of sustainability, and for shepherding human action through the labyrinth of environmental complexity. The environment is a fragile system that masks its own critical points, so that human incapacity and blindness cause failure to detect in time the vulnerability threshold below which natural systems can collapse. Unfortunately the ecological debt that environmental systems accumulate as a consequence of growing human destabilization is like a Sword of Damocles for the future of the entire Earth. This debt can be reduced and/or neutralized by the suggestion of new models of social and economic development where nonhuman organisms receive more respect and dignity from policymakers and stakeholders.

References

Abram, D. 2012. The spell of the sensuous: Perception and language in a more-than-human world. Vintage.

Adams, F. 2003. The information turn in philosophy. Minds and Machines 13: 471–501.

Alatalo, R.V., Gustafsson, L., Linden, M., Lunderberg, A. 1985. Interspecific competition and niche shifts in tits and the goldcrest: an experiment. Animal Ecology. 54: 977–984. https://doi.org/10.2307/4391

Allen, T. F., Starr, T. B. 1982. Hierarchy: perspectives for ecological complexity. University of Chicago Press.

Allen, T.F.H., Hoekstra, T.W. 1992. Toward a unified ecology. Columbia University Press, New York, US.

Appleton, J. 1996. The experience of landscape. Revised edition. Wiley & Sons, New York, NY, US.

Au, W. W. 1993. The sonar of dolphins. Springer Science & Business Media.

Ausonio 2015. La Mosella e altre poesie. Fabbri Centauria, Milano, IT.

Backhaus, G. 2006. An introduction to the conceptual formation of ecoscapes. Ecoscapes: Geographical Patternings of Relations. Oxford: Lexington Books.

Barber, J.R., Crooks, K.R., Fristrup, K.M. 2010. The costs of chronic noise exposure for terrestrial organisms. Trend Ecol. Evol. 25: 180–189.

Barbieri, M. 2003. The organic codes. Cambridge University Press, Cambridge, UK.

Barbieri, M. 2008. Biosemiotics: a new understanding of life. Naturwissenschaften, 95(7): 577–599. doi: 10.1007/s00114-008-0368-x.

Barbieri, M. 2019. A general model on the origin of biological codes. Biosystems, 181: 11–19.

Barrett, T.L., Farina, A., Barrett, G.W. 2009. Aesthetic landscapes: an emergent component in sustaining societies. Landscape Ecology 24: 1029–1035.

Bateson, G. 1970. Form, substance, and difference. General Semantic Bulletin 37: 5–13.

Battin, J. 2004. When good animals love bad habitat. Ecological traps and the conservation of animal populations. Conservation Biology, 18(6): 1482–1491.

Beavers, A.F. 2016. A brief introduction to the philosophy of information. Logeion: Filosofia da informacao, Rio de Janeiro, v. 3(1): 16–28.

Betts, M.G., Hadley, A.S., Rodenhouse, N., Nocera J.J. 2008. Social information trump's vegetation structure in breeding-site selection by migrant songbird. Proceedings of the Royal Society B. 275: 2257–2263. https://doi.org/10.1098/rspb.2008.0217

Bigerelle, M., & Iost, A. 2000. Fractal dimension and classification of music. Chaos, Solitons & Fractals, 11(14): 2179–2192.

Bissonette, J. (ed.) 1997. Wildlife and landscape ecology. Effects of patterns and scale. Springer, New York, US.

Blondel, J. 2006. The "design" of Mediterranean landscapes: a millennial story of human and ecological systems during the historic period. Hum Ecol 34: 713–729.

Blondel, J., Aronson, J. 1999. Biology and Wildlife of the Mediterranean Region. Oxford University Press, Oxford.

Blumenrath, S.H., Dabelsteen, T. 2004. Degradation of great tit (*Parus major*) song before and after foliation: implications for vocal communication in a deciduous forest. Behaviour. 141: 935–958.

Both, C., Grant, T. 2012. Biological invasions and the acoustic niche: the effect of bullfrog calls on the acoustic signals of white-banded tree frog. Biology Letters. 8: 714–716. https://doi.org/10.1098/rsbl.2012.0412

Bourassa, S.C. 1991. The aesthetics of landscape. Belhaven Press, London, UK.

Bradbury, J.W., Vehrencamp, S.L. 1998. Principles of animal communication. Sunderland, MA: Sinauer.

Breasted, J.H. 1905. A history of Egypt from the Earliest Times to the Persian Conquest. Havard University, Scribner.

Brown, L.R. 1975. The world food prospect. Science 190: 1053–1059.

Brown, L.R. 1981. World population growth, soil erosion, and food security. Science 214: 995–1002.

Brown, T.J., Handford, P. 2000. Sound design for vocalizations: quality in the woods, consistency in the fields. The Condor. 102: 81–92. https://doi.org/10.2307/1370409

Buchanan, K.L., Catchpole, C.K., Lewis, J.W., Lodge, A. 1999. Song as indicator of parasitism in the sedge warbler. Anim. Behav. 57: 307–314.

Buchanan, K.L., Spencer, K.A., Goldsmith, A.R., Catchpole, C.K. 2002. Song as an honest signal of past developmental stress in the European starling (*Sturnus vulgaris*). Proc. R. Soc. Lond. Ser. B Biol. Sci. 270: 1149–1156.

Buchler, J. 1955. Philosophical writings of Peirce. Dover Publication, Inc., New York, NY, US.

Busnel, R-G. 1968. Acoustic communication. In: Sebeok, T.A. (ed.), Animal communication. Indiana University Press, IN. pp. 127–153.

Cain, R., Jennings, P., Poxon, J. 2013. The development and application of the emotional dimensions of a soundscape. Appl. Acoust. 74: 232–239.

Carson, R. 1962. Silent Spring. Peguin Books.

Catchpole, C.K., Slater, P. 2008. Bird song. University Press, Cambridge.

Clements, F.E., Shelford, V.E. 1939. Bio-ecology. John Wiley & Sons, New York, NY, US.

Costanza, R., d'Arge, R., De Groot, R., Farber, S., Grasso, M.,Hannon, B., Limburg, K., Naeem, S., O'neill, R.V., Paruelo, J., et al. 1997. The value of the world's ecosystem services and natural capital. Nature 387: 253–260.

Cristancho, S., Vining, J. 2004. Culturally-defined keystone species. Review in Human Ecology, 11: 153–164.

Crutzen, P., Stoermer, E. 2000. The Anthropocene, global change. IGBP Newsl. 41, 17–18.

Curry, C.M., Des Brisay, P.G., Rosa, P., Koper, N. 2018. Noise source and individual physiology mediate effectiveness of bird songs adjusted to anthropogenic noise. Sci. Rep. 8: 3942.

Dale, V.H., Crisafulli, C.M., Swanson, F.J. 2005. 25 years of ecological change at Mount St. Helens. Science 308: 961–962. doi: 10.1126/science.1109684.

Dall, S.R.X., Johnstone, R.A. 2002. Managing uncertainty: information and insurance under the risk of starvation. Phil. Trans. R. Soc. London B. 357: 1519–1526

Dall, S.R.X., Houston, A.I., McNamara, J.M. 2004. The behavioural ecology of personality: consistent individual differences from an adaptive perspective. Ecology Letters 7: 734–739.

Dall, S.R.X., Giraldeau, L.A., Olsson, O., McNamara, J.M., Stephens, D.W. 2005. Information and its use by animals in evolutionary ecology. TREE 20(4): 187–193.

Danchin, E., Giraldeau, L-A. , Valone, T.J., Wagner, R.H. 2004. Public information: from nosy neighbors to cultural evolution Science 305: 487–491.

Darwin, C. 1859. The origin of the species. Murray, London, UK.

Delibes, M., Gaona, P., Ferreras, P. 2001. Effects of an attractive sink leading into maladaptive habitat selection. The American naturalist 158: 277–285.

Dennison, P.E., Brewer, S.C., Arnold, J.D., Moritz, M.A. 2014. Large wildfire trends in the western United States, 1984–2011, Geophys. Res. Lett., 41: 2928–2933. doi: 10.1002/2014GL059576.

Derryberry, E.P. 2009. Ecology shapes birdsong evolution: variation in morphology and habitat explains variation in white-crowed sparrow song. American Naturalist. 174: 24–33. https://doi.org/10.1086/599298

Derryberry, E.P., Danner, R.M., Danner, J.E., Derryberry, G.E., Philips, J.N., et al. 2016. Patterns of song across natural and anthropogenic soundscapes suggest that white- crowned sparrows minimize acoustic masking and maximize signal content. PLoS ONE. https://doi.org/10.1371/journal .pone.0154456

Diamond, J., Case, T.J. (eds.) 1986. Community ecology. Harper & Row, New York, US.

Di Castri, F. 1981. Mediterranean-type shrublands of the world. In: Di Castri, F., Goodall, D.W., Specht, R.L. (Eds.), Collection Ecosystems of the World, vol. 11. Elsevier, Amsterdam, pp. 1 /52.

Dorado-Correa, A., Goerlitz, H., Siemers, B.M. 2013. Interspecific acoustic recognition in two European bat communities. Frontiers in Physiology. 26 (4): 192. https://doi.org/10.3389/fphys.2013.00192

Dukas, R. (ed.) 1998. Cognitive ecology. The University of Chicago Press, Chicago, Il, US.

Dwernychuk, L.W., Boag, D.A. 1972. Ducks nesting in association with gulls. An ecological trap? Can. J. Zool. 50: 559–563.

Eder, J., Rembold, H. 1992. Biosemiotics – A paradigm of biology. Naturwissenschaften 79: 60–67.

Embleton, T.F.W. 1963. Sound propagation in homogeneous deciduous and evergreen woods. The Journal of the Acoustic Society of America. 35: 1119–1125. https://doi.org/10.1121/1.1918662

Eyring, C.F. 1946. Jungle acoustics. The Journal of Acoustical Society of America. 18 (2): 257–270. https://doi.org/10.1121/1.1916362

Fallow, P.M., Magrath, R.D. 2010. Eavesdropping on other species: mutual interspecific understanding of urgency information in avian calls. Animal Behaviour. 79: 411–417. https://doi.org/10.1016/j.anbehav.2009.11.018

Farina, A. 1993. Editorial comment: From global to regional landscape ecology. Landscape Ecology 8: 153–154.

Farina, A. 1998. Principles and methods in landscape ecology. Chapman & Hall, London, UK.

Farina, A. 2000. Landscape Ecology in Action. Kluwer Academic Publisher, Dordrecht

Farina, A. 2006a. Il paesaggio cognitivo. Una nuova entità ecologica. Franco Angeli, Milano.

Farina, A. 2006b. Principles and methods in landscape ecology. Springer, Dordrect, NL.

Farina, A. 2008. The landscape as a semiotic interface between organisms and resources. Biosemiotics 1: 75–83.

Farina, A. 2012. A biosemiotic perspective of the resource criterion: Toward a general theory of resources. Biosemiotics 5: 17–32. https://doi.org/10.1007/s12304-014–9213-0

Farina, A. 2014. Soundscape Ecology. Dordrecht: Springer. 315 pp.

Farina, A. 2018a. Perspectives in ecoacoustics: A contribution to defining a discipline. Journal of ecoacoustics 2, #TRZD5I. https://doi.org/10.22261/JEA.TRZD5I

Farina, A. 2018b. Rural sanctuary: an ecosemiotic agency to preserve human cultural heritage and biodiversity. Biosemiotics 11: 139–158.

Farina, A. Hong, S.K. 2004. A theoretical framework for a science of landscape. In: S.K. Hong, J.E. Lee, B.S. Ihm, et al. (eds.). Ecological issues in a changing world. Status, response and strategy. Kluwer, Dordrecht. Pp. 3–13.

Farina, A., Morri, D. 2008. Source-sink e eco-field: ipotesi ed evidenze sperimentali. Atti del X congresso nazionale della SIEP-IALE. Ecologia e governance del paesaggio: esperienze e prospettive. Bari, 365–372.

Farina, A., Pieretti, N. 2014. Acoustic codes in action in a soundscape context. Biosemiotics 7 (2): 321–328.

Farina, A., James, P. 2016. Acoustic community structure and dynamics: a fundamental component of ecoacoustics. Biosystems. 147: 11–20.

Farina, A., Johnson, A.R., Turner, S.J., Belgrano, A. 2003. "Full" world versus "empty" world paradigm at the time of globalization. Ecological Economics 45: 11–18.

Farina, A., Pieretti, N., Piccioli, L. 2011. The soundscape methodology for long-term bird monitoring: A Mediterranean Europe case-study. Ecol. Inform. 6, 354–363.

Farina, A., Pieretti, N., Salutari, P., Tognari, E., Lombardi, A. 2016. The application of the acoustic complexity indices (ACI) to ecoacoustic event detection and identification (EEDI) modeling. Biosemiotics. 9: 227–246. https://doi.org/10.1007/s12304-016–9266-3

Farina, A., Gage, S.H. 2017. Ecoacoustics: a new science. In: Ecoacoustics. The Ecological Role of Sounds, edited by Farina A. and Gage S.H. Oxford, UK: Wiley. 1–11.

Farina, A., Bogaert, J., Schipani, I. 2005. Cognitive landscape and information: new perspectives to investigate the ecological complexity. Biosystems 79 (1–3): 235–240.

Farina, A., Pieretti, N., Morganti, N. 2013. Acoustic patterns of an invasive species: the Red-billed Leiothrix (Leiothrix lutea Scopoli 1786) in a Mediterranean shrubland. Bioacoustics. 22: 175–194.

Farina, A., Gage, S.H., Salutari, P. 2018. Testing the ecoacoustics event detection and identification (EEDI) model on Mediterranean soundscapes. Ecological Indicators. 85: 698–715. https://doi.org/10.1016/j.ecolind.2017.10.073

Farina, A., Righini, R., Fuller, S., Li, P., & Pavan, G. 2020. Acoustic complexity indices reveal the acoustic communities of the old-growth Mediterranean forest of Sasso Fratino Integral Natural Reserve (Central Italy). Ecological Indicators, 120, 106927.

Floridi, L. 2010. Information: A very short introduction. Oxford University Press, Oxford, UK.

Forman, R.T.T., Godron, M. 1986. Landscape ecology. Wiley & Sons, New York, US.

Forman, R.T.T. 1995. Land mosaics. The ecology of landscapes and regions. Cambridge Academic Press, Cambridge, UK.

Foucher de Careil, L.A. 1859–1860. Ouvres inédit de Descartes. Lagrange et Durand, 1: 2–57.

Fourier, J. B. J. 1822. Théorie analytique de la chaleur. F. Didot.

Fraccascia, L., Giannoccaro, I., & Albino, V. (2018). Resilience of complex systems: state of the art and directions for future research. Complexity, 2018.

Francis, C.D., Ortega, C.P., Cruz, A. 2009. Noise pollution changes avian communities and species interactions. Current Biology. 19: 1415–1419. https://doi.org/10.1016/j.cub.2009.06.052

Gell-Mann, M. 1995. What is complexity? Complexity 1(1).

Gell-Mann, M., Lloyd, S. 1996. Information measures, effective complexity, and total information. Complexity, 2(1): 44–52.

Gibson, J.J. 1986. The ecological approach to visual perception: Erlbaum Associates, Inc. Hillsdale, N.J., US.

Gobry, I. 1959. St. Francois d'Assise et l'esprit franciscain. Edition du Seuil, FR

Golley, F. 1993. A history of the ecosystem concept in ecology. Yale University Press, New Haven US.

Griffin, D.R. 1959. Echoes of bats and men. Anchor Books.

Griffin, D.R., Hopkins, C.D. 1974. Sound audible to migrating birds. Anim. Behav. 22: 672–678.

Grime, J.P. 1973. Competitive exclusion in herbaceous vegetation. Nature 242: 244–247.

Grinnell, J. 1917. The niche relationship of the California thrashers. The Auk 34: 427–433.

Grove, A.T., Rackham, O. 2001. The Nature of Mediterranean Europe. An Ecological History, Yale University Press, New Haven and London

Gutzwiller, K.J., Anderson, S.H. 1992. Interception of moving organisms: influence of patch shape, size, and orientation on community structure. Landscape Ecology 6: 293–303.

Haber, W. 2004. Landscape ecology as bridge between ecosystems to human ecology. Ecological Research 19: 99–106.

Haines-Young, R., Potschin, M. 2010. The links between biodiversity, ecosystem services and human well-being. Ecosystem Ecology: a new synthesis, 1, 110–139.

Hale, R., Swearer, S.E. 2017. Ecological traps: current evidence and future directions. Proceedings of the Royal Society of London. Series B, 283, 20152647.

Hallmann, C.A., Sorg, M., Jongejeans, E., Siepel, H., Hofland, N., Schwan, H., Stenmans, W., Muller, A., Sumser, H., Horren, T., Goulson, D., de Kroon, H. 2017. More then 75 percent decline over 27 years in total flying insect biomass in protected areas. PLoS ONE 12(10):e0185809s

Hanski, I. 1999. Metapopulation ecology. Oxford University Press, Oxford, UK.

Healy, S. 1998. Spatial representation in animals. Oxford University Press, Oxford, UK.

Hoffmeyer, J. 1996. Signs of meaning in the universe. Indiana University Press, Bloomington, IN, US.

Hoffmeyer, J. 2008. The semiotic niche. Journal of Mediterranean Ecology 9: 5–30.

Holland, M.M., Risser, P.G., Naiman, R.J. (eds.) 1991. Ecotones. The role of landscape boundaries in the management and restoration of changing environments. Chapman & Hall, London, UK.

Holt, R.D. 2008. Theoretical perspective on resource pulse. Ecology 89(3): 671–681.

Hsü, K. J. 1993. Fractal geometry of music: From bird songs to Bach. In Applications of Fractals and Chaos (pp. 21–39). Springer, Berlin, Heidelberg.

Hutchinson, G.E. 1957. Concluding remarks. Cold Spring Harbor Symp 22: 415–427.

Hutchinson, G.E. 1978. An introduction to population ecology. Yale University Press, New Haven, CT, US.

Ingold, T. 2000. The perception of the environment. Routledge, Taylor and Francis Group, London, UK.

Jenkins, R. (2002). The Human World and the Natural World. In Foundations of Sociology (pp. 111–138). Palgrave, London.

Jones, M. 1991. The elusive reality of landscape. Concepts and approaches in landscape research Norsk. Geogr. Tidsskr. 45: 229–244.

Kaplan, R., Kaplan, S. 1989. The experience of nature. A psychological perspective. Cambridge University Press, Cambridge, UK.

Kitzberger, T., Falk, D. A., Westerling, A. L., & Swetnam, T. W. 2017. Direct and indirect climate controls predict heterogeneous early-mid 21st century wildfire burned area across western and boreal North America. PloS one, 12 (12), e0188486.

Kolasa, J., Pickett, S.T.A. (eds.) 1968. Ecological Heterogeneity. Springer-Verlag, New York, US.

Kolasa, J., Pickett, S.T.A. (eds.) 1991. Ecological Heterogeneity. Springer-Verlag, New York, US.

Kopnina, H. 2016. Half of the earth for people (or more)? Addressing ethical questions in conservation. Biological Conservation, 203, 176–185.

Krause, B.L. 1993. The niche hypothesis. Soundscape Newsletter. 6: 6–10.

Krause, B.L. 2012. The Great Animal Orchestra: Finding the Origins of Music in the World's Wild Places. London, England: Profile Books Limited. 277 pp.

Kroodsma, D.E. 2004. The diversity and plasticity of birdsong. In: Nature's Music, edited by Marler P. and Slabbekoorn H. Elsevier Academic Press, Cambridge, Massachusetts, US. 108–131.

Kull, K. 2005. Semiosphere and a dual ecology: paradoxes of communication. Sign Systems Studies 33, 175–189.

Laland, K.N., Brown, G.R. 2006. Niche construction, human behavior, and the adaptive-lag hypothesis. Evolutionary Anthropology, 15, 95–104.

Lemon, R.F., Struger, J., Lechowicz, M.J., and Norman, R.F. 1981. Song features and singing heights of American warblers. Maximization or optimization of distance? The Journal of the Acoustical Society of America. 69: 1169–1176. https://doi.org/10.1121/1.385697

Lepart, J., Debussche, M. 1992. Human impact on landscape patterning: Mediterranean examples. In Hansen, A.J., and di Castri, F. (eds.), Landscape Boundaries. Consequences for Biotic Diversity and Ecological Flows. Springer, Berlin Heidelberg New York, pp. 76–106.

Levins, R. 1968. Evolution in changing environments. Princeton University Press, Princeton, New Jersey, US.

Lewin, R. 1999. Complexity. Life at the edge of chaos. 2nd ed., The University of Chicago Press, Chicago, Il, US.

Lidicker Jr, W. Z. (2008). Levels of organization in biology: on the nature and nomenclature of ecology's fourth level. Biological Reviews, 83(1),71–78.

Lindstrom, K., Kull, K., Palang, H. 2011. Semiotic study of landscapes: an overview from semiology to ecosemiotics. Sign System Studies 39(2): 12–36.

Lindstrom, K., Palang, H., Kull, K. 2014. Landscape semiotics. Lang, V., Kull, K. (eds). Estonian Approaches to Culture Theory. Approaches to Culture Theory 4, 110–132. University of Tartu Press, Tartu.

Lister, B.C., Garcia, A. 2018. Climate-driven declines in arthropod abundance restructure a rainforest web. PNAS 115, 44, E10397-E10406.

Lloyd, S. 1990. The calculus of intricacy. The Sciences, 30 (5): 38–44.

Lloyd, S. 2007. Programming the universe. A quantum computer scientist takes on the cosmos. Vintage Books, London, Uk.

Lodge, D.J., McDowell, W. 1991. Summary of ecosystem-level effects of Caribbean hurricanes. Biotropica 23(4a): 373–378.

Luther, D., Gentry., K. 2013. Sources of background noise and their influence on vertebrate acoustic communication. Behaviour, 150: 1045–1068.

MacArthur, R.H., Wilson, E.O. 1967. The theory of island biogeography. Princeton University Press, Princeton, US.

Magrath, R.D., Haff, T.M., Fallow, P.M., Radford, A.N. 2014. Eavesdropping on heterospecific alarm calls: from mechanisms to consequences. Ecological Review. 90: 560–586. https://doi.org/10.1111/brv.12122

Maran, T., Kull, K. 2014. Ecosemiotics: main principles and current developments. Geografiska Annaler: Series B, Human Geography 96 (1): 41–50.

Maran, T., Martinelli, D., Turovski, A. (Eds.). 2011. Readings in zoosemiotics (Vol. 8). Walter de Gruyter.

Maran, T., Tønnessen, M., Magnus, R., Mäekivi, N., Rattasepp, S., Tüür, K. (2016). Introducing zoosemiotics: philosophy and historical background. Tartu Semiotics Library 18, 10.

Marten, K., Marler, P. 1977. Sound transmission and its significance for animal vocalization. Behavioral Ecology and Sociobiology. 2: 271–290. https://doi.org/10.1007/BF00299740

McGregor, P.K., Dabelsteen, T. 1997. Communication network. In Ecology and Evolution of Acoustic Communication in Birds; Kroodsma, D.E., Miller, E. H., Eds. Cornell University Press: Ithaca, NY, US; pp. 409–425.

Menant, C. 2003. Information and meaning. Entropy 5: 193–204.

Merry, U. 1995. Coping with uncertainty: Insight from the new science of chaos, self-organization, and complexity. Praeger Publishers, Westport, CT, US.

Miller, N.F. 1992. The origins of plant cultivation in the Near East. In Cowan, C. W. , and Watson, P.J. (eds.), The Origins of Agriculture: An International Perspective, Smithsonian, Washington, District of Columbia, pp. 39–58.

Mislan, K.A.S., Heer, J.M., White E.P. 2016. Elevating the status of code in ecology. Trends in Ecology & Evolution. 31: 4–7. https://doi.org/10.1016/j.tree.2015.11.006

Monacchi, D., Farina, A. 2019. A multiscale approach to investigate the biosemiotics complexity of two acoustic communities in primary forests with high ecosystem integrity recorded with 3D sound technologies. Biosemiotics, 12 (2): 329–347.

Mönkkönen, M., Helle, P., Soppela, K. 1990. Numerical and behavioral responses of migrant passerines to experimental manipulation of resident tits (Parus spp): heterospecific attraction in northern breeding communities. Oecologia. 85: 218–225. https://doi.org/10.1007/BF00319404

Morley, R.J. 2000. Origin and evolution of tropical rain forests. John Wiley & Sons, Chichester, UK.

Morton, E. 1975. Ecological sources of selection on avian sounds. The American Naturalist. 109 (965): 17–34. https://doi.org/10.1086/282971

Morton, E.S. 1987. The effects of distance and isolation of song-type sharing in the Carolina wren. Wilson Bull. 99(4): 601–610.

Morton, E.S., Gish, S.L., van der Voort, M. 1986. On the learning of degraded and underdegraded songs in the Carolina Wren. Anim. Behav. 34: 815–820.

Moscoso, P., Peck, M., Wibberley, S., Eldridge, A. 2018. A systematic cross-disciplinary literature review on the association between soundscape and ecological/human wellbeing. PeerJ 6, e6570v2.

Muller, K.L., Stamps, J.A., Krishnan, V.V., Willits, N.H. 1997. The effects of conspecific attraction and habitat quality on habitat selection in territorial birds (*Troglodytes aedon*). The American Naturalist 150(5): 650–661.

Mullet, T.C., Farina, A., Gage, S.H. 2017. The acoustic habitat hypothesis: an ecoacoustics perspective on species habitat selection. Biosemiotics, doi: 10.10007/s12304-017-9288-5.

Naguib, M., Wiley, R.H. 2001. Estimating the distance to a source of sound: mechanisms and adaptations for long-range communication. Animal Behaviour 62: 825–837.

Naguib, M., Klump, G. M., Hillmann, E., Grießmann, B., & Teige, T. 2000. Assessment of auditory distance in a territorial songbird: accurate feat or rule of thumb?. *Animal Behaviour*, 59(4): 715–721.

Nassauer, J.I. 1995. Culture and changing landscape structure. Landscape Ecology 10: 229–237.

Naveh, Z. 1974. Effects of fire in the Mediterranean region. In Kozlowski, T.T., and Ahlgren, C.E. (eds.), Fire and Ecosystems, Academic, New York, pp. 401–434.

Naveh, Z. 1994. The role of fire and its management in the conservation of Mediterranean ecosystems and landscapes. In Moreno, J.M., and Oechel, W.

C. Eds., The Role of Fire in Mediterranean-Type Ecosystems,Springer, Berlin Heidelberg New York, pp. 163–185.

Naveh, Z. 2003. What is holistic landscape ecology? A conceptual introduction. Landscape and Urban Planning 50: 7–26.

Naveh, Z., Lieberman, A. 1996. Landscape ecology. Theory and application, 2nd edition. Springer-Verlag, New York, NY, US.

Odling-Smee, J., Douglas, H.E., Palkovacs, E.P., Feldman, M.W., Laland, K.N. 2013. Niche construction theory: a pratical guide for ecologists. The Quarterly Review of Biology 88: n.1.

Odum, E.P. 1959. Fundamentals of ecology. 2d ed. W.B. Saunders, Philadelphia, US.

Odum, H.T. 1983. System ecology. John Wiley & Sons, Inc., New York, NY, US.

Paine, R.T. 1966. Food web complexity and species diversity. The American Naturalist 100: 65–75.

Paine, R.T. 1969. A note on trophic complexity and community stability. American Naturalist 103: 91–93.

Paine, R.T. 1995. A Conversation on Refining the Concept of Keystone Species. Conservation Biology. 9 (4): 962–964. doi: 10.1046/j.1523-1739.1995.09040962.x.

Papageorgiou, N. 1979. Population Energy Relationships of the Agrimi (Capra Aegagrus Cretica) on Theodorou Island, Paul Parey Verlag, Hamburg and Berlin, DE.

Parmentier, E., Berten, L., Rigo, P., Aubrun, F., Nedelec, S.L., Simpson, S.D., Lecchini, D. 2015. The influence of various reef sounds on coral fish larvae behavior. J. Fish Biol. 86: 1507–1518.

Patten, B.C., Auble, G.T. (1981). System theory of the ecological niche. The American Naturalist, 117(6),893–922.

Pianka, E.R. 1970. "On r and K selection" (PDF). American Naturalist. 104 (940): 592–597. doi: 10.1086/282697.

Pianka, E.R. 1986. Ecology and natural history of desert lizards. Princeton University Press, Princeton, NJ, US.

Pickett, T.A., White, P. (eds.) 1985. The ecology of natural disturbance and patch dynamics. Academic Press, Orlando, FL, US.

Pieretti, N., Farina, A., Morri, D. 2011. A new methodology to infer the singing activity of an avian community: The Acoustic Complexity Index (ACI). Ecological Indicators 11: 868–873.

Pijanowski, B.C., Villanueva-Rivera, L.J., Dumyahn, S.L. Farina, A., Krause, B. L., Napoletano, B.M., Gage, S.H., Pieretti, N. 2011a. Soundscape ecology: The science of sound in the landscape. Bioscience 61(3). 203–216.

Pijanowski, B.C., Farina, A., Gage, S.H., Dumyahn, S.L., Krause, B.L. 2011b. What is soundscape ecology? An introduction and overview of an emerging new science. Landscape Ecology 26(9). 1213–1232.

Plumwood, V. 2006. The concept of a cultural landscape: Nature, culture and agency in the land. Ethics and the Environment 11 (2): 115–150.

Pulliam, R. 1988. Sources-sinks, and population regulation. American Naturalist 132: 652–661.

Radford, C.A., Stanley, J.A., Jeffs, A.G. 2014. Adjacent coral reef habitats produce different underwater sound signatures. Mar. Ecol. Prog. Ser. 505: 19–28

Ratcliffe, J.M., Nydam, M.L. 2008. Multimodal warning signals of a multiple predator world. Nature, 455, 96–99.

Reading, A. 2011. Meaningful information: the bridge between biology, brain, and behavior. SpringerBriefs in Biology 1, doi: 10.1007/978–1-4614–0158-2_2. Springer Science+Business Media, LLC.

Real, L.A., Brown, J.H. (eds) 1991. Foundations of ecology. The University of Chicago Press, Chicago, US.

Real, L.A. 1993. Toward a cognitive ecology. TREE 8(11): 413–417.

Reba, M., Reitsma, F., Seto, K.C. 2016. Spatializing 6,000 years of global urbanization from 3700 BC to AD 2000. Scientific Data, 3, 160034.

Risser, P.G., Karr, J.R., Forman, R.T.T. 1984. Landscape ecology: Directions and approaches. Special Publication Number 2, 18 pp, Illinois Natural History Survey, Champaign, IL, US.

Sal, A., Belmontes, J-A., Nicolau, J-M. 2003. Assessing landscape values: a proposal for a multidimensional conceptual model. Ecological Modelling 168: 319–341.

Sanchez-Bayo, F., Wyckhuys, K.A.G. 2019. Worldwide decline of the entomo-fauna: a review of its drivers. Biological Conservation 232: 8–27.

Sauer, C.O. 1925. The morphology of landscape. University of California Press, Berkeley, CA.

Saussure, F. de 2011. Course in general linguistic. Columbia University Press.

Scheiner, S.M., Willig, M.R. 2005. A general theory of ecology. Theoretical Ecology. doi: 10.007/S12080-007-0002.0.

Scheiner, S.M., Willig, M.R. 2011. The theory of ecology. The University of Chicago Press.Chicago, Il, US.

Schrodinger, E. 1944. What is life. The physical aspect of the living cell. Cambridge University press, Cambridge, UK.

Schwinning, S., Sala, O.E. 2004. Hierarchy of responses to resource pulses in arid and semiarid ecosystems. Oecologia 141: 211–220.

Sebastian-Gonzalez, E., Hart, P.J. 2017. Birdsong meme diversity in a fragmented habitat depends on landscape and species characteristics. Oikos. 126: 1511–1521. https://doi.org/10.1111/oik.04531

Secretariat of the Convention on Biological Diversity 2010. Global Biodiversity Outlook 3. Montréal, 94.

Sebeok, T. A. 1965. Animal Communication: A communication network model for languages is applied to signaling behavior in animals. *Science, 147*(3661): 1006–1014.

Shannon, C. 1948. A mathematical theory of communication. Bell System Technical Journal 27: 379–423 & 623–656.

Shannon, C.E. 1993. Collected Papers, edited by N.J.A. Sloane and A. D. Wyner, IEEE Press, New York, NY, US.

Shannon, G., Angeloni, L.M., Wittemyer, G., Firstrup, K.M. 2014. Road traffic noise modifies behaviour of a keystone species. Animal Behaviour. 94: 135–141. https://doi.org/10.1016/j.anbehav.2014.06.004

Siegenfeld, A.F., Bar-Yam, Y. 2019. An Introduction to Complex Systems Science and its Applications. arXiv preprint arXiv:1912.05088.

Simberloff, D. 1998. Flagships, umbrellas, and keystones: is single-species management passé in the landscape era?. *Biological conservation, 83*(3): 247–257.

Sirot, E., Renaud, P. C., & Pays, O. 2016. How competition and predation shape patterns of waterhole use by herbivores in arid ecosystems. Animal Behaviour, 118: 19–26.

Smith, M. (2014). Deep ecology: what is said and (to be) done?. The Trumpeter, 30(2), 141–156.

Stephens, D.W., Krebs, J.R. 1986. Foraging theory. Princeton University Press, Princeton, NJ, US.

Stewart, O.C. 2002. Forgotten fires: Native Americans and the transient wilderness. OK, US: Univ. of Oklahoma Press. p. 364. ISBN 978–0806140377.

Stonier, T. 1996. Information as a basic property of the universe. BioSystems 38, 135–140.

Strong, D.R., Frank, K.T. 2010. Human involvement in food webs. Annual review of environment and resources, 35, 1–23.

Sueur, J. 2018. Sound Analysis and Synthesis with R; Springer: New York, NY, US

Sueur, J., Farina, A. 2015. Ecoacoustics: the ecological investigation and interpretation of environmental sound. Biosemiotics 8: 493–502. https://doi.org/10.1007/s12304-015-9248-x

Sueur, J., Farina, A., Gasc, A., Pieretti, N., Pavoine S. 2014. Acoustic indices for biodiversity assessment and landscape investigation. Acta Acustica United with Acustica 100: 772–781. https://doi.org/10.3813/AAA.918757

Suzuki, T.N. 2012. Long-distance calling by the Willow Tit, Poecile montanus, facilitates formation of mixed species foraging flocks. Ethology 118: 10–16.

Templeton, J.J., Giraldeau, L.-A. 1995. Patch assessment in foraging flocks of European starling: evidence for the use of public information. Behav. Ecol. 6: 65–72.

Tilley, C. 1994. A phenomenology of landscape. Berg Publishers, Oxford, UK.

Towsey, M., Znidersic, E., Broken-Brow, J., Indraswari, K., Watson, D., Phillips, Y., Truskinger, A., Roe, P. 2018. Long-duration, false-colour spectrograms for detecting species in large audio data-sets. Journal of Ecoacoustics, 2.

Treccani 2020. http://www.treccani.it/vocabolario/santuario/

Turner M.G. (ed.) 1987. Landscape heterogeneity and disturbance. Springer-Verlag, New York.

Turner, M.G. 1989. Landscape ecology: the effect of pattern on process. Annu. Rev. Ecol. Syst. 20: 171–197.

Turner, M.G., Gardner, R.H., O'Neill, R.V. 2001. Landscape ecology in theory and practice. Pattern and process. Springer-Verlag, New York, US.

UNFPA 2020. http://www.unfpa.org/urbanization

Vale, T.R. (ed.). 2002. Fire, Native Peoples, and the Natural Landscape. Island Press, Washington, DC, US.

Valone, T.J., Templeton, J.J. 2002. Public information for the assessment of quality: a widespread social phenomenon. Phil. Trans. R. Soc. London B 357: 1549–1557.

van Droste, B., Plachter, H., Rossler, M. (Eds.) 1995. Cultural Landscapes of Universal Value. Gustav Fischer, Jena.

Varela, F., Maturana, H. 1980. Autopoiesis and Cognition: the Realization of the Living. Reidel.

Vining, J., Merrick, M.SD., Price, E.A. 2008. The distinction between human and nature: human perceptions of connectedness to nature and elements of the natural and unnatural. Human Ecology Review 15: 1–11.

Vladimorova, E., Mozgovoy, J. 2003. Sign field theory and tracking techniques used in studies of small carnivorous mammals. Evolution and Cognition 9(1): 73–89.

von Barwise, J., Seligman, J. 1997. Information flow: The logic of distributed systems. Cambridge: Cambridge University Press, Cambridge, UK.

von Uexküll, J. 1926. Theoretical biology. London: Kegan, Paul, Trench, Trubner and Company Ltd.

von Uexküll, J. 1982(1940). The theory of meaning. Semiotica 42: 25–82.

von Uexküll, J. 1992(1934). A stroll through the worlds of animals and men. Semiotica 89 (4): 319–391. https://doi.org/10.1515/semi.1992.89.4.319

Wang, R., Downton, P., Douglas, I, 2010. Towards ecopolis. New technologies, new philosophies and new developments. In: Douglas, I., Goode, D., Houck, M., Maddox, D. (Eds.). (2010). Handbook of urban Ecology. Routledge. Pp. 636–651.

Ward, P., Zahavi A. 1973. The importance of certain assemblages of birds as "information- centres" for food-finding. Ibis 115: 517–534. https://doi.org/10.1111/j.1474-919X.1973.tb01990.x

Wheatcroft, D., Price, T.D. 2015. Rates of signal evolution are associated with the nature of interspecific communication. Behavioral Ecology. 26 (1): 83–90. https://doi.org/10.1093/beheco/aru161

White, L. 1967. The historical roots of our ecologic crisis. Science, 155 (3767),1203–1207.

Wiener, N. 1948. Cybernetics: or control and communication in the animal and the machine. John Wiley & Sons, New York.

Wu, J., Hobbs, R.J. (eds) 2007. Key topics in landscape ecology. Cambridge University Press, Cambridge, UK.

Yang, L.H., Bastow, J.L., Spence, K.O., Wright, A.N. 2008. What can we learn from resource pulse? Ecology 89(3): 621–643.

Cambridge Elements ≡

Environmental Humanities

Louise Westling
University of Oregon

Louise Westling is an American scholar of literature and environmental humanities who was a founding member of the Association for the Study of Literature and Environment and its president in 1998. She has been active in the international movement for environmental cultural studies, teaching and writing on landscape imagery in literature, critical animal studies, biosemiotics, phenomenology, and deep history.

Serenella Iovino
University of North Carolina at Chapel Hill

Serenella Iovino is Professor of Italian Studies and Environmental Humanities at the University of North Carolina at Chapel Hill. She has written on a wide range of topics, including environmental ethics and ecocritical theory, bioregionalism and landscape studies, ecofeminism and posthumanism, comparative literature, eco-art, and the Anthropocene.

Timo Maran
University of Tartu

Timo Maran is an Estonian semiotician and poet. Maran is Professor of Ecosemiotics and Environmental Humanities and Head of the Department of Semiotics at the University of Tartu. His research interests are semiotic relations of nature and culture, Estonian nature writing, zoosemiotics and species conservation, and semiotics of biological mimicry.

About the Series

The environmental humanities is a new transdisciplinary complex of approaches to the embeddedness of human life and culture in all the dynamics that characterize the life of the planet. These approaches reexamine our species' history in light of the intensifying awareness of drastic climate change and ongoing mass extinction. To engage this reality, Cambridge Elements in Environmental Humanities builds on the idea of a more hybrid and participatory mode of research and debate, connecting critical and creative fields.

Cambridge Elements ⁼

Environmental Humanities

Printed in the United States
By Bookmasters